Augsburg Commentary
on the New Testament

Augsburg Publishing House
Minneapolis, Minnesota

Library of Congress Cataloging in Publication Data

Smith, Robert H., 1932-
  HEBREWS.

  (Augsburg commentary on the New Testament)
  Bibliography: p. 183
  1. Bible. N.T. Hebrews—Commentaries. I. Title.
II. Series.
BS2775.3.S65   1984   227'.8707   83-72125
ISBN 0-8066-8876-9

Manufactured in the U.S.A.   APH 10-9034

1   2   3   4   5   6   7   8   9   0   1   2   3   4   5   6   7   8   9

The unknown author of Hebrews labels his own work
"a word of encouragement." It is fitting to dedicate
this commentary on Hebrews to a churchman and educator
who has by his courage and personal sacrifices
encouraged my ministry and indeed made it possible
for my ministry and that of countless colleagues to continue.
To
John H. Tietjen
for his ministry of encouragement.

CONTENTS

ABBREVIATIONS

BAGD	Walter Bauer, *A Greek-English Lexicon of the New Testament and Other Early Christian Literature,* trans. and adapted by W. F. Arndt, F. W. Gingrich, and F. W. Danker (2nd ed.; Chicago: University of Chicago, 1979).
HTR	*Harvard Theological Review*
IDB	*The Interpreter's Dictionary of the Bible,* ed. G. Buttrick (5 vols.; Nashville: Abingdon, 1962, 1976).
JBL	*Journal of Biblical Literature*
KJV	King James Version
LXX	The Septuagint
NTS	*New Testament Studies*
RSV	Revised Standard Version
TDNT	*Theological Dictionary of the New Testament,* ed. G. Kittel and G. Friedrich, trans. G. Bromiley (10 vols.; Grand Rapids: Eerdmans, 1964-1976).
TEV	Today's English Version of the Bible.

FOREWORD

The AUGSBURG COMMENTARY ON THE NEW TES-
TAMENT is written for laypeople, students, and pastors. Laypeople will use it as a resource for Bible study at home and at
church. Students and instructors will read it to probe the basic
message of the books of the New Testament. And pastors will
find it to be a valuable aid for sermon and lesson preparation.

The plan of each commentary is designed to enhance its
usefulness. The Introduction presents a topical overview of the
biblical book to be discussed and provides information on the
historical circumstances in which that book was written. It
may also contain a summary of the biblical writer's thought.
In the body of the commentary, the interpreter sets forth in
brief compass the meaning of the biblical text. The procedure
is to explain the text section by section. Care has also been
taken to avoid scholarly jargon and the heavy use of technical
terms. Because the readers of the commentary will have their
Bibles at hand, the biblical text itself has not been printed
out. In general, the editors recommend the use of the Revised
Standard Version of the Bible.

The authors of this commentary series are professors at
seminaries and universities and are themselves ordained clergy-
persons. They have been selected both because of their exper-
tise and because they worship in the same congregations as the
people for whom they are writing. In elucidating the text of

Scripture, therefore, they attest to their belief that central to the faith and life of the church of God is the Word of God.

The Editorial Committee

Roy A. Harrisville
Luther Northwestern Theological Seminary
St. Paul, Minnesota

Jack Dean Kingsbury
Union Theological Seminary
Richmond, Virginia

Gerhard A. Krodel
Lutheran Theological Seminary
Gettysburg, Pennsylvania

INTRODUCTION

A recent discussion of Hebrews begins with the observation that the King James Version of the Bible entitles our document "The Epistle of Paul the Apostle to the Hebrews" and continues with the declaration that the modern consensus contradicts that title point by point. Our document is not an epistle, not by Paul nor by any other apostle or eyewitness, and not addressed to a specifically Hebrew audience.[1] In that case, what can be said positively about the author, the form or genre of the document, the time of composition, and the situation of the readers?

■ Paul, the Author of Hebrews?

From the end of the fourth century down to the Reformation, the majority opinion was that Hebrews was quite simply the 14th epistle of the apostle Paul. Up until the second half of the fourth century, however, Roman and western writers generally denied the letter to Paul and did not list it in the canon of sacred and authoritative writings. In part, western opposition to Hebrews rested on the judgment that its teaching on the impossibility of repentance and forgiveness for sins committed after Baptism (see 6:4-6; 10:26-31) was both un-Pauline and wrong.

9

On the other hand, eastern Christians from an early date held Paul to be the author. Pantaenus (d. ca. A.D. 200), the founder of the Christian school at Alexandria, apparently accepted Hebrews as Paul's. His pupil, Clement of Alexandria (d. ca. A.D. 215), regarded the Greek literary style as akin to that of the third gospel and the Acts of the Apostles and concluded that Paul had written the document in Hebrew and that Luke had translated it into Greek.

Clement's pupil and successor, Origen (d. ca. A.D. 255), was the greatest scriptural scholar of the ancient church. He judged Hebrews to be admirable both in thought and in the expression of the thought. The Greek style is not that of Paul, who, Origen recalled, acknowledged himself to be "rude in speech" (2 Cor. 11:6 KJV). The diction of Hebrews is purer Greek.[2]

Furthermore, the content or teaching of Hebrews was to the mind of Origen in no way inferior to the acknowledged apostolic writings. Origen concluded that Hebrews was produced by someone (he suggested Luke or Clement of Rome) who remembered the apostolic teachings and wrote them down at his leisure. He understood why "the ancients" transmitted Hebrews as Paul's, but he himself concluded, "Who authored the epistle truly God alone knows." [3]

Origen was prepared to live with a non-Pauline Hebrews, but the majority could not. The view eventually prevailed that Paul was the author, and that opinion held sway down to the time of the Reformation, when many church traditions were subjected to critical scrutiny. The Dutch humanist Erasmus, Cardinal Cajetan, and Martin Luther—so unlike and such fierce opponents on so many issues—found themselves in unaccustomed agreement on the authorship of Hebrews: "Not by Paul." John Calvin prized Hebrews as apostolic but agreed that it was not from the pen of Paul.

But if Paul did not write Hebrews, who did?

1. Barnabas, suggested already by Tertullian (ca. 155-220), has proved an attractive possibility because of his Levitical

background, his residence in Jerusalem (dominated by the temple), and his association with Paul and his independence from him (Acts 9:27; 11:22-30; 12:25–13:2; 15:1-40; Gal. 2:13). His very name means "son of exhortation" or "son of encouragement" (Acts 4:36), and Hebrews is "a word of exhortation" (13:22). Barnabas continues to be named by people who seek a Jewish-Christian author intimate with the details of temple ritual.

2. Apollos was proposed originally by Martin Luther, and he has had his champions ever since. He was close enough to Paul, indoctrinated by converts of Paul, and yet he was independent enough to be a rival of Paul and speak with his own accent. Moreover, he had the required rhetorical skill and intellectual power (Acts 18:24-28; 1 Cor. 1:12; 3:4-9; 16:12). He is the kind of person favored by those who are convinced that the author must have been a convert from the sort of Hellenistic Judaism represented by Philo of Alexandria.

3. Luke was named by Clement of Alexandria and has been nominated also in recent times by people who are impressed especially by the linguistic similarities between Luke-Acts and Hebrews, by the way these writings seem to them to be dominated by a vision of the ongoing history of God's people, and by the manner in which the old and new covenants are linked by the scheme of promise and fulfillment.

4. Priscilla was proposed by Adolf von Harnack at the turn of the century. After all, she along with Aquila was tutor to Apollos (Acts 18:26). She and Aquila were associated with Timothy, named in Hebrews 13:23 (cf. Acts 18:2; 19:22; 1 Cor. 16:10, 19), and they were also resident in Rome (Rom. 16:3; cf. Heb. 13:24). Priscilla enjoys some vogue among those seeking biblical role models for contemporary women and biblical challenges for old-fashioned men.[4]

■ Our Author's Unique Outlook

Many modern discussions of Hebrews begin accurately enough with the declaration that Paul did not write Hebrews, but then proceed to fill technical terms in Hebrews with Pauline contents and to interpret the whole of Hebrews as though it were after all the 14th letter of the apostle. The effort must be made to let Hebrews be Hebrews and to permit its distinctive voice to be heard.

Of course Hebrews and Paul's letters have much in common, and a list of themes from Hebrews makes it easy to see why many have upheld the tradition of Pauline authorship: centrality of God as Maker and Creator; Jesus Christ as the pre-existent Son of God and agent of creation; the impotence of the law as instrument of salvation; the vast difference between the covenants signified by Mount Sinai and the heavenly Jerusalem; the finality and centrality of Jesus' death in God's dealings with an errant humankind; the strong accent on the obedience of Christ; Jesus as present Lord, high and exalted over all things; and the imminent denouement of human and cosmic history.

But, on the other hand, Paul and the author of Hebrews speak differently of law and faith. Paul tends to regard the law in rabbinic fashion, as embodying God's will for the conduct of every aspect of personal and social life, while Hebrews views the law almost entirely in terms of its cultic connections and expressions: the law established the sanctuary, the priesthood, and the sacrificial system (see commentary on 2:2 and 7:11).

Paul never describes Jesus as great high priest, the primary image in the christological presentation of Hebrews, and Hebrews is completely innocent of Paul's unique and central teaching on the church as the body of Christ and on believers as being "in Christ" or "in Christ Jesus."

For Paul, faith is acceptance of the gift God has already granted in Jesus Christ, while for Hebrews, faith projects itself out into the future and upwards to the invisible world as hope and endurance (see commentary on 4:2; 10:37; and 11:1-2).

Hebrews is also un-Pauline in other noteworthy respects. The basic pattern of Paul's thought is historical and eschatological. He has a grand and sweeping vision of the march of history. It begins with primeval times and the rebellion of Adam and continues through God's promise to Abraham, the declaration of the law through Moses, and the testimony of prophets, to the climax and goal of all God's dealings with people in Jesus. For the moment everything seems to proceed as before, but in truth, Paul indicates, history has caught its breath at the stunning crescendo worked in Jesus' death and resurrection, and the grand finale of history will occur speedily. This will include the last day, the resurrection of all the dead, the final judgment, and the subjection of all things to God, who will be all in all.

But the author of Hebrews does not think his thoughts within that kind of historical framework. That he was familiar with that way of thinking is not disputed. But Hebrews exhibits another pattern of thought. The dominant pattern is spatial rather than historical, and the horizontal dualism of before and after is overshadowed by the vertical dualism of above and below.

The dualism of Hebrews has been called Platonic. That is not to say that the author had read Plato's dialogs or attended the Academy in Athens, but that as an inhabitant of the Hellenistic world he shared the kind of thinking associated with the name and influence of the continuing Platonic tradition. It was one of several "modern" (from his point of view) assumptions about the nature of the world. It stressed that the actual things of this world are only copies of transcendent ideas or forms.[5]

Hebrews seems indebted to this Platonic heritage in its continual contrasting of the things of creation and the things of heaven. Things below, the things of the world or this creation, are manifold and varied, like the revelation through the prophets. They are temporal, transitory, unstable, and perishing, and that description applies even to angels and to the heavens as part of God's creation (Hebrews [1]). By contrast, the superior realities of heaven above are one or unified, abiding, enduring, and eternal, like the revelation in the Son. The Lord is the same and his years never end (1:12), and Jesus is the same yesterday and today and forever (13:8).

The Levitical priests are many, weak, mortal, and earthly, offering repeated sacrifices at a shrine made with hands, which is an imitation or copy, a mere shadowy reproduction upon the earth of the true and original shrine made by the Lord in heaven. Their sacrifices gain only temporary relief or an external benefit. Jesus, however, is a great high priest of an altogether different order of reality. He is one and singular, marked by indestructible life, permanent, exalted above the heavens to the celestial sanctuary. There he has offered a single sacrifice once for all, valid eternally, gaining eternal redemption touching not the body only but the conscience and innermost self (7:1–10:18).

Faith is the perception of the reality and stability of the unseen (11:3) and means keeping one's heart fixed not on the possession of the land of Canaan or an earthly city, but on a continuing and abiding city, a city with foundations, a better heavenly country (11:10-16; 13:14). Believers have come not to another Mount Sinai, shakable and touchable, but to the heavenly Jerusalem, intangible and stable, to Jesus and to God himself (12:18-24).

Of course our author, for all his dualism and affinity with Platonic modes of thought, knows that the spiritualizing habit of that world view has been shattered at crucial points. He insists on Jesus' sharing our flesh and blood in the incarnation, on the stubborn reality of Jesus' temptations and sufferings, and on the everlasting power of Jesus' death. For him, the movement of the faithful toward their heavenly rest is not simply the progress of disembodied souls making individual ascents. It is rather the corporate ascent of the community of pilgrim people spanning the generations.

■ Time of Writing

Dating New Testament documents is a notoriously slippery business. Hebrews is harder to date by far than Romans or 1 Corinthians, since the latter were indubitably by Paul, and Paul's career can fairly accurately be traced on a map and a calendar with the aid of clues given in his own writings and in the Acts of the Apostles. But Hebrews is an anonymous document and offers hardly a hint concerning the time of its publication.

Of course if the author were Paul, Luke, Apollos, Priscilla, or Barnabas, then we could make a good stab at dating, but these names are guesses at best.

Many have declared rather overconfidently that the arguments of Hebrews assume that the Jewish temple was still standing at the time of composition. We know that it was razed when Jerusalem was stormed by the Romans in A.D. 70. Therefore, it is asserted, Hebrews must have been composed prior to the year 70.

But does Hebrews really presuppose that the temple was still in active use? At least two arguments can be advanced against that conclusion.

In the first place, the author of Hebrews has not fixed his eye on Herod's temple fabricated of stone or on the priests of his own day entering the sanctuary repeatedly. He has pondered rather the ancient pre-Solomonic tabernacle and its rituals as they are described in the Pentateuch. The focus of his theological meditation is not history but a text, not the contemporary status quo in Jerusalem but the verbal depiction of tabernacle and ritual contained in sacred scripture (see commentary on 9:1-5).

But could he have written as he has if the temple lay in ruins? Even after A.D. 70 the temple, priesthood, and ritual lived in the hearts and hopes of Jewish people. The coins of Bar Kochba minted during the second revolt of A.D. 132–135 bear the image of the temple facade as if it stood unmoved on its platform. The *Mishnah* compiled by Rabbi Judah around A.D. 200 contains innumerable directions and decisions regarding temple, priests, holy days, and sacrifices, as though they were all in force.

To our author the toppling of Jerusalem's temple and the cessation of sacrifice were reasons for neither despair nor gloating. He neither hoped for their restitution, nor did he point people to an alternative Christian temple establishment with a Christian priesthood and Christian liturgy. He stands firm against any and all priestly, sacrificial, ritualistic traditions with sacred sites, sacred times, and sacred acts—whether Jewish, pagan, or Christian.

The word of Jesus in John 4:23 might serve as our author's own slogan in these matters: "The hour is coming, and now is, when the true worshipers will worship the Father in spirit and truth."

Certainly the author and his readers were not numbered among the original eyewitnesses but had received the good news from their predecessors in the faith who had seen and heard Jesus (2:1-4; cf. Luke 1:1-4). They were members of the second or third generation of Christians, not the first. On the other hand, our document must not be dated too late in the first century, since Clement of Rome, writing around A.D. 96, knew Hebrews and alluded to it (1 Clement 17:1, 5; 36:1-5).

The view adopted in the present work is that Hebrews was probably penned after the fall of Jerusalem and the destruction of the temple, perhaps in the 80s of the first century.

■ The Situation of the Author and First Readers

It is frustrating to have to admit with Origen that "God alone knows" who wrote Hebrews. We all know that people keep trying to identify the author. The impetus behind the continuing quest is not sheer stubbornness or mere curiosity. It is rather the conviction that certain mysteries surrounding the writing would be cleared up if the author could be identified with certainty.

If only we knew the author's name, the date and place of his birth, the schools he attended, the books he read, the names of his parents and teachers and co-workers, the historical path he personally traveled, the cities he visited, the boundaries he crossed both literally in journeys and figuratively in his spiritual and intellectual development, the major events in the church and the empire during his life, then we would obviously be in a stronger postition as we approach The Letter to the Hebrews.

It would likewise help to know the first readers addressed so powerfully and passionately by our author. Who are these people? Can they be located geographically, chronologically, socially, ethnically, religiously? What was their economic and political standing?

Sometime in the second century our document received the title "To the Hebrews." That name is on the one hand an admission of ignorance and on the other hand a guess. Documents regularly bore the name of the city to which they were sent: "to the Colossians," "to the Corinthians." Evidently Hebrews was not associated with any specific geographical place. Those who first named the document guessed that the talk about sacrifices, priests, and sanctuary must have been directed to people fascinated by such matters, perhaps Jewish-Christians tempted to return to Judaism with its ritual system.

However, the author never uses the words *Jews* or *Christians*. Indeed this familiar distinction is foreign to his outlook. One of his high hopes is that his readers will prove to be in real continuity and community with the faithful heroes of the past, Hebrews as well as non-Hebrews, like Abel, Enoch, Noah, and Melchizedek. He does not argue against attachment to circumcision or dietary laws but rather deplores attachment to the earth, to things created, made with hands and so passing away. He seeks to strengthen his readers for continuing on their pilgrims' way by reminding them of the cloud of witnesses (mostly Jewish) surrounding them.

The author says to his readers that "those who come from Italy send you greetings" (13:24), and that most naturally indicates that the writing is directed to people in Italy. That the readers are urged to greet their fellow saints (13:24) indicates that the document was directed to some one special set among the totality of believers in the place. The readers may be a particular group or single house church of Roman Christians of mixed Jewish and Gentile background living sometime in the second half of the first century.

But these hints are so vague as to be meaningless. A better course is to pay close attention to the text and milk it not just for clues to the readers' names, dates, and geographical places but for evidence regarding their spiritual situation. The following profile results.

The readers were veterans in the faith and not mere neophytes or recent converts. Some of their original teachers and leaders had died (13:7), and the author can remind them of that and of other events in their Christian past which are likely to slip from memory because of the passage of years. He alludes to charismatic activity in their midst on the occasion of their coming to faith: "signs and wonders and various miracles and . . . gifts of the Holy Spirit" (2:4). He speaks frequently of their "confession" (3:1; 4:14; 10:23)—perhaps a creed learned and boldly confessed at the time of their initiation into the community. In addition he calls upon them to remember how they gladly suffered abuse from the non-Christian public in the past and how they had reacted in those harsh circumstances (10:32-34). They had displayed an astonishing love toward one another in those early days and had loved one another nobly. They had never lost any blood to persecution (12:4), and the hardest trials were past. Nevertheless, some of the company still languished behind bars, and it was dangerous to identify with them publicly (13:3). Furthermore, readers were liable to be abused simply for being Christian (13:3). Neither hardship nor heroism are past, but love and care are mentioned as cooling (6:10).

The fires of their original enthusiasm have been banked and the coals of their mutual affection glow more faintly now. They quite simply have grown tired. They are victims of listlessness and have become sluggish of spirit (6:11-12), like runners overcome by exhaustion and loss of willpower a far distance from the finish line (12:1, 3, 12). They are not holding fast their initial confidence. Instead, second thoughts are creeping in and robbing them of their energy and boldness (3:14).

Part of their trouble is that they have stopped growing, and yet they seem oblivious or indifferent to their arrested development and stunted growth. They are stuck at the level of beginners, babies in the faith, and they do not care about hearing, learning, and progressing to maturity. Growth to maturity and attaining the goal require a practical discipline of which they seem incapable (5:11—6:2; 12:1-17). With exhortation of this kind our author tries to shame his readers.

Another of our author's strategies, in addition to shaming his readers with a description of their malaise, is to utter warnings, striking for their severity. He uses the strongest possible language as he contemplates their inattentiveness to God's speech in Jesus, their waning boldness, and their loss of patient endurance.

He warns that his readers are in danger of losing all they had gained by confessing their faith and entering the community in the first place. If their carelessness were to continue, they might even be swept away from salvation by the floodwaters (2:1-3). They teeter on the edge of a whirlpool of unbelief, rebelliousness, and disobedience. If they fall in, they will fail to enter God's promised rest (3:12-19).

They need to open their ears and hearts to the word by which the community lives (2:3; 4:1-2; 5:11; 12:25) and listen attentively to their leaders, including the author (13:17-19,

22). Some have cut themselves off from the fellowship of Christian brothers and sisters, placing themselves beyond the reach of the word, neglecting the assembly, and so depriving themselves of the benefits of mutual encouragement (10:25; 3:13).

If they do not open their ears, if they become deaf to God's word, they will be guilty of spurning the Son of God, profaning the blood of the covenant, and outraging the Spirit of grace (10:29). They will be found making common cause with the crucifiers of Jesus and will be among those who treat Jesus with utter contempt (6:6). They may fall away from the living God (3:11) and fall into the hands of the living God (10:31). That is to say, apostasy brings in its train a fearful prospect of judgment.

Those images of rebellion and apostasy have led many to conclude that the author and his readers were involved in some fierce doctrinal dispute. Perhaps the readers, if Jewish-Christians, were tempted to relapse into Judaism and to depend once again on the rituals of the Levitical priesthood. Or perhaps the readers, whether former Jews or Gentiles, were attracted by some amalgam of Christian and Jewish or pagan ideas about angels.

Time and again students of Hebrews, fascinated by the comparison between the Son and angels in the opening chapters, have suggested that the readers were tempted by a false teaching like the one scored by Paul in the letter to the Colossians. The Christians at Colossae are warned about a philosophy which is really an empty deceit concocted by the human imagination. The elemental spirits of the universe, also called principalities and powers, held an honored place in that scheme, and adherents indeed actually worshiped those angelic beings and submitted to their ordinances and demands (Col. 2:8-23).

Paul responded by reminding the Colossians of the incomparable greatness of Jesus, the unique Son of God, describing him in terms reminiscent of the opening of Hebrews and declaring his superiority over all powers both visible and in-

visible, including thrones, dominions, principalities, and authorities—names for various classes of angels and spirits (Col.
1:15-20).

However, the notion that our author has in view some
false philosophy or heresy cannot be sustained. If Hebrews
were a polemic directed at an antithetical teaching or religious system, then it might be expected to include some sharp
lashing out at Jewish or pagan opponents outside the church
or at gullible dupes or false teachers within. It should name
Pharisees, scribes, or other leaders of the synagogue in the
days beyond the destruction of the temple at Jerusalem in
A.D. 70, or grapple with the Sadducees or Pharisees over the
relative merits of sacrifice and priesthood at the Jerusalem
sanctuary in the days immediately before destruction. We
would expect a recoiling from concrete proposals regarding
the worship of angels or the giving of honors due solely to
Christ to principalities and powers or to prophets, priests, and
Moses. We should encounter a summary of a vain philosophy,
a Jewish ordinance or error, or a half-Christian doctrine or
heresy powerfully tugging at their loyalty. But none of this
is present in Hebrews.

The readers have gone slack and grown weary. They are
in danger of a great fall, not because they are exchanging one
fervently held conviction (the true one) for another (the false
one). They have not traded a new love for an old one. Their
old love has simply cooled. Danger posed by fascination with
a heresy or false religion simply does not connect with the
spiritual condition of the readers as our author has described
it.

Our author's diagnosis of his readers' condition is that they
are suffering from an acute case of lethargy. Indeed, he declares that their sluggishness or weariness has reached crisis
proportions. But he does more than pronounce a diagnosis
and utter warnings. Our author sets before his readers magnificent promises. If they will but rouse themselves and endure
in faith, then they will obtain eternal salvation, be in God's

house, enter God's rest, receive mercy, find grace in every time of need, attain perfection, enter the heavenly sanctuary, receive a city with foundations or a better heavenly country and homeland. They will draw near to the throne of grace and see the Lord.

■ The Form and Structure of Hebrews

Hebrews is one of the premier documents of encouragement in all of Christian history. The unknown author viewed with apprehension a rising tide of lassitude and lethargy among his readers. By the exercise of his very considerable rhetorical and intellectual gifts he set himself the task of constructing a dike against that swelling flood.

Hebrews is not a letter, in spite of its traditional title. It lacks most of the marks of an epistle. It does not open with an epistolary prescript, with salutation naming the recipients and the sender and greeting them with peace and grace. Nor does it continue with a thanksgiving, rehearsing the relations between readers and author and serving as a kind of table of contents or index to the concerns filling the writing. The document does conclude as letters ordinarily do with final greetings and conventional phrases about prayer, peace, and travel plans.

The body of the composition is not arranged in the typical fashion of a Pauline letter. Paul ordinarily developed doctrinal materials in the opening chapters of his letters and then, when his theological exposition was complete, he turned to ethical exhortation.

Hebrews is frequently forced into a Pauline mold and read as though doctrinal concerns were not only uppermost in the mind of the author but also dominant in his exposition, with exhortations tacked onto the end and playing a decidedly subordinate role. Such outlines label the materials in 10:19—13:25, or only the materials in Chapter 13, as ethical and hortatory. But Hebrews is not a Pauline letter, nor is it a polemical tract or doctrinal treatise.

Our author's strategy in meeting the challenge posed by his readers' spiritual lethargy was to compose a unique "word of exhortation" (13:22), the name he himself affixes to his composition. Exhortation or encouragement, the lifting of drooping hands and the emboldening of faint hearts, is our author's highest priority.

Of course our author expounds a high doctrine. His exposition of Jesus' priesthood is a stunning intellectual achievement. But the point of all his argumentation—the reason for his explication of solid doctrinal food, the word hard to explain, the word of righteousness (5:11-14)—is thoroughly practical. The encouragement he offers is rooted in tough thinking and considered teaching. His theological exposition is in the service of ethical exhortation. By declaring the incomparable greatness of Jesus and of what is the Christian's in and through him, our author grounds his exhortation on solid theological underpinnings.

It has been argued above that our author's mental habits or basic disposition can be described as Platonic and that he has pondered the status and significance of Jesus in an altogether fresh and intellectually challenging fashion. However, it is also true that his heritage is thoroughly Christian. He not only reproduces the Christian tradition but also quotes bits and pieces of Christian creeds, acclamations, and hymns. It is clear that his purpose in marshaling his arguments, in ransacking the tradition, in quoting and alluding, in crafting and shaping his phrases, and in his heady innovating and pathfinding is thoroughly practical. He prods and probes, exposes and warns, quotes and argues in order to encourage.

The following outline attempts to exhibit our author's habit of keeping a steady eye on his readers' practical needs, and to show how from the beginning he displays before them reasons of the mind interwoven with reasons of the heart.

OUTLINE OF HEBREWS

I. Give Heed to the Word Spoken in Jesus! (1:1—4:13)
  A. Prolog: God Has Spoken in One Who Is Son (1:1-4)
  B. Exposition: He Is Superior to Angels (1:5—2:18)
    1. Angels Are Transitory Servants (1:5-14)
    2. First Exhortation: Pay Closer Attention! (2:1-4)
    3. He Became Pioneer of Salvation and Merciful High Priest (2:5-18)
  C. Exposition: He Is Superior to Moses (3:1—4:10)
    1. He Was Faithful over God's House as Son (3:1-6)
    2. Hardness of Heart Excluded Moses' Generation from God's Rest (3:7-19)
    3. There Remains a Sabbath Rest for the People of God (4:1-10)
  D. Concluding Exhortation: Strive to Enter that Rest! (4:11-13)

II. Let Us Hold Fast Our Confession! (4:14—10:31)
  A. Opening Exhortation: Let Us Hold Fast Our Confession of Jesus as Priest! (4:14-16)
  B. Opening Exposition: Jesus Is High Priest after the Order of Melchizedek (5:1-10)
    1. Appointed Priest by God (5:1-6)
    2. He Learned Obedience (5:7-10)

COMMENTARY

Give Heed to the Word Spoken in Jesus! (1:1—4:13)

■ Prolog: God Has Spoken in One Who Is Son (1:1-4)

The opening of Hebrews is credal, hymnic, and solemn, lacking the identifying marks of an epistle. As impressive and artful as the preface to Luke (Luke 1:1-4), it resembles even more the prolog to John (John 1:1-18), not only in its liturgical style but even in its content.

In Luke's preface, as in that of the intertestamental book of Sirach, the history of God's people passes in swift review, climaxing in a statement about the writer as self-conscious author or publisher. On the other hand, the authors of Hebrews and John remain hidden, and Jesus alone holds the stage as the revelation of God.

In Greek the initial paragraph is a single sentence, which, because of its complexity, the RSV has rendered with three separate English sentences. The following layout may help exhibit the concerns of the author. It follows the RSV as closely as possible except that it renders Greek relative pronouns and participles by English relative pronouns and participles in order to clarify the basic structure. The author composed the paragraph with skill and care so that every word and phrase carries weight. Some of his words are italicized simply as an aid in grasping what appears to be the essential core of thought which is then developed in the remainder of the work.

1. In many and various ways *God,* having spoken of old to our fathers by the prophets,
2. in these last days *has spoken to us by a Son* whom he appointed the heir of all things through whom also he created the world
3. *Who*
   being the reflection of the glory of God and the very stamp of his nature
   upholding the universe by his word of power *having made purification* for sins *sat down at the right hand* of the Majesty on high,
4. having become as much superior to angels as the name he has obtained is more excellent than theirs.

Speaking of the Son as the embodiment of God's Word has its close parallels in John's prolog, but the description of the Son as accomplishing the priestly work of purification is the peculiar property of Hebrews. Indeed one of the author's grand achievements is to present Jesus both as unique revealer and as unique priest.

1:1—In many and various ways God spoke of old to our fathers. Fathers is a traditional designation for the men and women of the elder covenant, emphasizing filial respect for them and continuity with them across the generations, in spite of all the discontinuity introduced by God's culminating action in Jesus (see especially Rom. 9:5; Acts 3:13; Sirach 44:1).

God spoke to them **in many and various ways.** Is this reference to multiplicity and variety a positive or negative assessment of past revelation? Both RSV and TEV seem to take it positively. The latter renders the opening phrase: "many times and in many ways." However the NEB captures the author's intended poignancy when it translates, "in fragmentary and varied fashion."

In the author's vocabulary *multiplicity* has about it the aroma of the earth and of the various senses by which we are related to the manifold things of the earth. Our senses draw us in many directions, yield a mixed picture of the world, fix our beings on the palpable things of the world, and easily lead to confusion, to drifting, to wandering. The heavenly world is marked in contrast by singularity, simplicity, wholeness, perfection, and stability. To behold that world with the eyes of faith means to be lifted above incompleteness and multiplicity and to begin to share in spiritual maturity or perfection.

The author sees much to praise in the revelation of the past. It serves as rich testimony to the community of the present (Chap. 11), and yet across that prior dispensation he writes the word *old*. The patriarchs and prophets belong to a time now suddenly made obsolete and antiquated (Heb. 8:13), marked by inconclusiveness and incompleteness, by comparison with the ultimacy and finality of what God has now given **in these last days** (Gen. 49:1; Num. 24:14; Deut. 31:29; Isa. 2:2; Dan. 10:14). **In these last days** is a phrase expressing the common Christian conviction of living in the time of consummation and fullness, bursting with possibilities of new life.

In days **of old** God addressed his people through dreams and signs, through vision and audition, in earthquake and storm, by Urim and Thummim, in bush and fire, in smoke and a column of cloud, through angels and even through animals. But most clearly, forcibly, and memorably God addressed the ancients **by the prophets.**

The word **prophets** is meant in the widest sense. In traditional Jewish nomenclature the books of the Old Testament we usually call "historical" (Joshua, Judges, Samuel, and Kings) are termed "the former prophets," and indeed the word **prophet** was applied to Abraham, Isaac, Jacob (Luke 13:28; Gen. 20:7), Moses (Deut. 34:10), Joshua (Sirach 46:1), and David (Acts 2:30), among other ancient spokesmen (see Ps. 105:15).

1:2—The total rich variety of God's disclosures and revelations in ancient times and the totality of his fresh action and manifestation in the birth and baptism, instructions and miracles, sufferings and resurrection of Jesus are all subsumed under the notion of God's "speech": **God spoke of old to our fathers** and **in these last days he has spoken to us.**

Through all his dealings with his people in the historical realities of their situation, God has been speaking. God is pictured as using that superb and subtle means of communication, instrument of deepest personal communion, binding heart to heart—the Word.

After all his previous communicating, God has done it again. God's new action is described as a Word, and this final Word, singular and decisive, came in one who bears the name and who is indeed quite simply **Son.**

Angels are the swift messengers of God; Abraham is the friend of God; Moses is the prophet on most intimate terms with God; Aaron is the first great high priest of God; many lived nobly generation after generation by faith in God; but Jesus is **Son,** unique and peerless.

No other name or title so clearly expresses the relationship between God and Jesus as the simple word *Son* borrowed from the intimacy of the family circle.

In early Christianity Jesus is the incomparable Son (Heb. 1:5; 5:5; 10:29), and others are called "sons" or "children" as a title of honor in a secondary or derived sense, as persons adopted into the family to stand alongside the one Son (cf. 2:10, 14, 17; 12:7, 9) who is elder "brother" in a great family of sisters and brothers.

Two clauses, encompassing the entirety of universal history from alpha to omega, further describe the Son. The first looks toward the end and goal of all world history: the Son is the one whom God has **appointed the heir of all things.** The second clause looks backwards in time to the genesis of all things: the Son is the one **through whom also** God **created the world.**

To Adam was given dominion over all things, but his dominion became misrule and abuse as he lapsed into distrust and disobedience. Human history can be read as a melancholy tale of greed and grabs for power by individuals and nations intent on enriching themselves and increasing their domain. The author, by his assertion about the Son, declares that the strong of the earth are presently impressive, but only the one Son has been **appointed the heir of all things**. Sonship and inheritance are inextricably linked (Rom. 8:17; Gal. 3:29). The future belongs to the one who is both Son and heir.[6]

Attempts to eliminate him are doomed to failure, no matter how successful they may appear to be for the moment (Mark 12:1-11). Here the author is signaling his readers to be careful lest they lose their share in the inheritance to come by forgetting the basics of their faith. The Son will one day displace all pretenders, and it will be seen that all things are his and all who belong to him will share in the inheritance with him (Heb. 2:10; Matt. 5:5; Gal. 4:7; Rom. 4:13; cf. Ps. 2:8).

That glorious goal has been prepared from the beginning. He is the one **through whom also** God **created the world**. Early Christianity taught that the agency of the divine action of creation and the God-given basis for an indestructible life with the Lord of the universe—everything which Judaism saw and revered in Torah (Law), Logos (Word), or Sophia (Wisdom)—was embodied in Jesus.

These two clauses (**appointed . . .** , **through whom . . .**), the content of which can be traced in many strata of the New Testament (John 1:3, 10; 1 Cor. 8:6; Col. 1:16), are so neat and precise in formulation that some have suspected that they are fragments of an early Christian creed. That may be so, but in any case they surely constitute a dike against all escapism or etherealizing of faith.

1:3—In verse 3 the subject of the clauses switches from God to the Son. We hear first what the Son always is and always has been in spite of all appearances to the contrary, then what he did during his work in history in Jesus. Finally and climactically we hear that he has taken his seat at God's right hand.

a) "Being": That he **reflects the glory of God** means not merely that he is moon and God is sun, or that he is a single ray of light among many streaming forth from God, but that he is the entire brilliant effulgence which sets before us the true light in all its splendor.

Furthermore, he **bears the very stamp of his nature,** as a coin bears the image of the ruler or as a statue sets before subjects not merely the neutral abstract likeness but the full and lively authority of the sovereign. Dishonoring the image is dishonoring the one represented. So both reflection and image are parables of relationship. The Son comes forth from God and sets the reality of God before people in full efficacy and authenticity (John 10:30; 14:8-9).

In pre-Christian traditions both Wisdom (Wisd. of Sol. 7:25-26) and Word or Logos (in Philo) were called effulgence and image of the invisible God.[7] But for Christians, Jesus is the final answer to the age-old questions: What is the mind of God? Where is the bridge or ladder to God? In the words, deeds, and sufferings of Jesus we are confronted with the passionate life of God himself. We do not see all of God in him, but all that we do see is true and genuine, without any distortion or deception.

b) "Upholding": But what does it mean that the Son is **upholding the universe by his word of power?** The Son is hardly being pictured like Atlas bent beneath the weight of the world upon his shoulders. A Jewish tradition teaches that the world rests upon three things: Torah, worship of God, and deeds of loving service (M. Pirqe Aboth 1:2). As the tranquility of the world and life itself are threatened by crime and evil (M. Pirqe Aboth 5:1), harmony and life are enhanced by these three, and indeed without them the world would relapse into chaos. The author of Hebrews is echoing the Christian conviction that the powers and energies resident in the Son are what keep the world from collapsing (cf. Heb. 11:3; Col. 1:17). That which sustains, upholds, and bears the world is not the law proclaimed on Sinai, not some esoteric knowledge granted to a spiritual elite, not wisdom available in the tradition of sages, and surely not political or financial clout, but only his **word of power,** the message declared at first by the Lord (2:3). People must attend to that if they are really to live.[8]

c) "Purifying": The author moves from images drawn from prophecy to others derived from priesthood. He shifts from speech to sacrifice, from revelatory word to **purification.**

Not a word is breathed here about Jesus' conception or birth, boyhood or baptism, teaching or miracles, or any other event from the days of his popularity. This fourth clause focuses wholly and entirely upon his death and exaltation taken as a single event. Both here and in the heart of Hebrews (Chap. 7–10) what we call Good Friday and Easter are interpreted as the great and final Day of Atonement (Leviticus 16) for the whole world. A death has occurred which has fully and forever removed the stain and burden of sin (cf. 2 Peter 1:9; 1 John 1:7).

d) "Sitting": Being effulgence and image, bearing all things, and having effected purification, **he sat down at the right hand of the Majesty on high.**

Here the clauses reach their climax in a paraphrase of Psalm 110, one of the most influential and beloved of all psalms in early Christianity.[9] It is used both here and at 1:13 and so provides the basic framework for the chain of passages presented in the intervening verses. By means of Psalm 110, Hebrews focuses on the exaltation of Jesus. Like Paul, the author of Hebrews speaks little of the life or ministry of Jesus and much of his death and its stunning and lively aftermath. However, while Paul celebrates the climax of Jesus' way in terms of resurrection, Hebrews rarely speaks of "resurrection," but prefers other terms and images.[10]

The author of Hebrews offers several closely related pictures of the goal of the way of Jesus through and beyond his death: he is exalted above the heavens (7:26), he has taken his seat at God's right hand (8:1; 10:12; 12:2), he has been installed as eternal high priest (2:17; 5:5-10), he has inherited a new name (1:4; 4:14).

The phrase **on high** both here and at 8:1 reveals the author's habit of thinking in spatial terms. Jesus is **on high** or in the heavenly and transcendent world, high above flux, change, and passing away.

1:4—He always was the Son (1:2; 5:8), but at his exaltation he received **the name** which is **more excellent** than that of angels, just as he really is **superior** to them. He has begun to be acclaimed as Son and his sonship has begun to have its effects upon humankind (cf. Rom. 1:3-4).

The author spells out the comparison with angels through the rest of Chapter 1 and through Chapter 2, but the point he is making is one that also engages him from beginning to end of his entire writing; namely, the revelation of the Old Testament, associated with the presence of angels, accomplished by their mediation, and issuing in the establishment of the Levitical priesthood, has been superseded and so made obsolete by the word God has now spoken in these last days in one who is Son. The superiority of the Son over the angels is signaled in **the name he has obtained.** In biblical parlance a name is an outward expression of inward reality. He has been given rank and power far surpassing that of angels. In the old hymn in Phil. 2:6-11, Jesus "was graced" by God with the name of "Lord," and here in Hebrews **he has obtained** or inherited from God the **name** of "Son." Both "Son" and "Lord" figure prominently in early Christian confessions and hymns.

■ Exposition: He Is Superior to Angels (1:5—2:18)

Angels Are Transitory Servants (1:5-14)

This new section is a catena (chain) or florilegium (bouquet) of seven biblical passages. Five of them come from the Psalms, a book for which the author has a special affection. Together they define the assertion of verse 4 that he has become

superior to the angels and that he has a **more excellent name.**
The section is more poetry than polemic, and at least as much
doxology as argument. It is an outburst both ecstatic and canny
in its commentary not only on verse 4 but on the whole of the
opening paragraph (1:1-4). In verse 14 the author descends
from the heights of his recollection of the poetry and prophecy
of former times and adds a prose comment linking the catena
to the next section, 2:1-4, as densely packed and carefully
worded as 1:1-4.

As a whole the section acclaims the Son as divine, unchanging, and eternal, while it describes angels by contrast as servants of God, mere creatures, belonging to the temporal and
passing order of things. The section prepares for all that follows about the everlastingness of the word of the Son and the
unshakeable and eternal validity of the new covenant in his
blood.

A More Excellent Name (1:5-6)

1:5—The anthology opens with a pair of passages on *Son*
chosen because they were classic embodiments of Israel's
hopes.

Kings of Israel on the day of their enthronement were
ritually adopted by God, a liturgical signal that they were not
self-appointed rulers but had been lifted by God to their high
rank and were under obligation to represent God's own justice
in their ruling: **Thou art my Son, today I have begotten thee**
(Ps. 2:7).

Lying behind Psalm 2 was the even more ancient oracle of
Nathan to David in 2 Sam. 7:14. When David planned to
crown his renewal of Jerusalem by constructing for God a
house or temple, God countered by declaring that he would
build a house or dynasty for David: **I will be to him a father,
and he shall be to me a son.**

Psalm 2 and other royal psalms expressed the conviction
that God's word through Nathan was coming true at least in
part at each successive coronation, and every enthronement

and its celebration roused expectations of renewal for the nation and indeed for the entire cosmos. The texts used on those occasions began to function independently of earthly enthronements. They fueled the hopes of the people for the coming of God's reign over his universe (Psalms of Solomon 17:23-26; 18:6-8; see also the Dead Sea Scroll 4 Q Florilegium).

In the early church the expectations enshrined in oracle and psalm were thought to have come true variously in Jesus' birth (Luke 1:32-33; 2:11, "today"), his baptism (Mark 1:11; Luke 3:21, note the variant reading), transfiguration (Mark 9:7; 2 Peter 1:17), crucifixion (Mark 15:39; Luke 23:43, "today"), or resurrection (Rom. 1:4; Acts 13:33). The letter to the Hebrews describes Jesus' installation as king-priest at the right hand of God as the moment when the ancient words achieved their destined fulfillment (Heb. 1:3-4; 5:5). His enthronement as Son inaugurates the great and final **today** (Ps. 95:7; Heb. 3:7; 4:7; cf. Luke 4:21).

Hebrews is not interested in demonstrating Jesus' connections with the house of David. It is vitally concerned to assert that Jesus is the unique and final Son of whom all previous rulers and priest-kings were pale imitations or foreshadowings. He is the true and eternal Son over all God's house (3:1-6).

Angels, on the other hand, were "sons" or "children" of God only in the sense of heavenly creatures (see Pss. 29:1; 89:6 in RSV), inhabiting God's house as his servants.

Hebrews has opened with a comparison between Jesus and prophets (1:1). Why has it shifted so swiftly to comparing Jesus with angels? One old answer is that the community he addresses was disturbed by a heresy featuring the adoration of angels, was holding an understanding of Jesus as an angelic being, or was failing to appreciate Jesus as Messiah.[11]

However, the author seems most concerned to compare the definitive word God has now spoken in the Son with the words previously mediated through angels (2:2). The angels represent the Torah and the entire old covenant, including especially all its cultic apparatus for dealing with sin.

All of that had a certain kind of validity and usefulness, but it could not and did not remove sin in any final or definitive fashion. The ancient word and the ancient cult were powerless to give full access to God but did perform a service as copies and shadows of the realities now exhibited in Christ.

1:6—The third quotation in the chain is from Deuteronomy. The first two texts say that Jesus alone is Son enthroned on high. This third is closely associated with the first two, insisting as they do that the Son enjoys absolute preeminence over the angels, but it flips the coin so that we see the other side.

The words introducing the quotation are not crystal clear: **when he brings the first-born into the world.** Who is **the first-born?** Which moment is it when **all God's angels worship him?** What **world** does he mean?

In Ps. 89:27 **first-born** is a prestigious title for the king of Israel in contrast to all other kings. Rabbis sometimes called the Law or Torah God's **first-born,** and for Philo the Word or Logos was **first-born.** But now that exalted title is applied to Jesus in his uniqueness as God's Son (Rom. 8:29; Gal. 1:15, 18; cf. Heb. 12:23). As applied to Jesus, it is very nearly a synonym of "beloved" (Mark 1:11) and "only-begotten" (John 1:18 KJV). All these terms express Jesus' unique closeness to the Father.

So Jesus is the **first-born,** but what moment of homage does the author have in view? Is he referring to the incarnation at Christmas (Luke 2:14)? More probably he means the Son's introduction to the heavenly **world,** the coming world (2:5), and the moment of his coronation in highest heaven.

As the Son was enthroned at God's right hand (1:3), the divine decree went out: **Let all God's angels worship him** and pay him homage (Deut. 32:43 LXX; Matt. 4:11). The conception that angels, authorities, and spiritual powers are subject to the Son and serve him is deeply embedded in primitive Christian tradition (Mark 1:13; Matt. 26:53; Luke 22:43; 1 Peter 3:22; Phil. 2:10-11; 1 Tim. 3:16; Revelation 4–5; Ascension of Isaiah 11:23ff.). Obviously he to whom homage is paid is the superior one, whose name and worth are more excellent than those of the worshipers.

The Son Rules for Ever (1:7-12)

The first three quotations concentrate on the relative value of the names "Son" and "angels" by declaring that the greater excellence of the Son consists in the fact that his rule belongs to the heavenly and hence eternal world, while angels are part of God's transitory creation designed not for dominion but for humble service.

1:7—The fourth biblical text, Ps. 104:4, says that God **makes his angels winds and his servants flames of fire** (cf. Acts 7:30; 2 Thess. 1:8). These words could mean that angels are elemental forces, swift and strong, but Hebrews uses this language to define angels as creatures every bit as unstable, insubstantial, and ephemeral as **winds** and **fire.** An ancient rabbinic source declares that "every day ministering angels are created from the fiery stream; they utter a song and perish." [12]

How different is the Son. God **makes his angels** and they belong to the created order, but the Son is source of creation (1:2; cf. 12:27) and is exalted on high. The angels come to be and pass away in a single day, but he is the same yesterday and today and forever (13:8).

1:8-9—The fifth (like the sixth) quotation features the permanence of the Son's rule. **Of the Son** but not of angels **he says, Thy throne, O God, is for ever and ever** (Ps. 45:6).

The psalm originally praised the king (Ps. 45:1) who sat upon a "divine throne," one guaranteed by the oath God swore in the promise he gave to David through Nathan (see commentary on 1:5).

Hebrews 1:8 might be translated, "God is your throne for ever," but *God* is probably vocative (an address) as is *Lord* in 1:10, and the author of Hebrews saw Psalm 45 as placing the Son on the divine and eternal side of reality (cf. Isa. 9:6, "Mighty God").

Not just in contrast to the kings of ancient Israel but in contrast to the angels (1:7), the Son holds the throne **for ever and ever,** as he is high priest for ever, continues for ever, is perfected and the same for ever (5:6; 6:20; 7:17, 21, 24, 28; 13:8).

Length of days, indeed eternity, characterizes the Son's rule, but our author uses the psalm also to remind his oppressed and weary readers that the Son rules in righteousness. His emblem is a **righteous scepter,** and he has **loved righteousness and hated lawlessness.**

His rule ushers in righteousness and in his presence is joy for evermore. The Son, seated at God's right hand, has already been anointed with the **oil of gladness** (Ps. 23:5; Isa. 61:3; Luke 4:18) and has arrived at joy (12:3) in advance of the **comrades** or community he leads, namely God's many other children (2:10-13).[13]

1:10—In the sixth text, Ps. 102:25-27, the poet in his affliction pours out his complaints before God and finds hope, not in the smoking wick of his own fleeting life, but in God's solid and enduring reality. The earth and the heavens and all that are in them are only **the work of thy hands** (cf. 9:11, 24). **They will perish,** but the Lord remains.

They will **all grow old like a garment,** wearing out like clothing, fit only to be discarded (Isa. 34:4; 50:9; 51:6; Sirach 14:17), but the Lord is **the same,** and his **years will never end.**

The Lord is the one through whom all things came to be (cf. 1:2), and he is seated now high above all creation. He alone is exempt from the universal law of aging and dying, and those who are the Lord's will arm themselves with that thought (2:14-15; cf. Ps. 16:8-11 in Acts 2:25-28).

Sit at My Right Hand (1:13)

1:13—The seventh text, Ps. 110:1, climaxes the series and completes a circle as it explicitly quotes the verse which is only alluded to in 1:3. To the Son, to him alone and to no angel, God has said, **Sit at my right hand, till I make thy enemies a stool for thy feet.**

Christ is enthroned in highest heaven. The author is indirectly but forcibly addressing his readers' lassitude and faltering in faith, whether caused by the excitement of persecution or the tedium of an uneventful pilgrimage. They need a bracing reminder of the Son's supreme and eternal position within the whole scheme of things.

Psalm 110:1 was much used in the early church. One of our author's great contributions to Christian thought and devotion derives from the simple fact that he read past verse 1 down to verse 4: "Thou art a priest for ever." He used that verse as the basis for his assertion that Christ is eternal high priest after the order of Melchizedek (5:6; 7:1—10:18).

Ministering Spirits (1:14)

1:14—The author wraps his bouquet of poetic and oracular passages in a prose comment. Angels are **all ministering spirits.** In the letter to the Hebrews angels have a very restricted role to play. They are not portrayed as standing in the presence of God offering sacrifice or chanting his glory. Heavenly intercession and sacrifice are the work of the Son. They do not wage war in heaven against the powers of darkness, nor do they function as guardians of the nations or of defenseless children. In Hebrews, angels run swiftly through the universe to do God's bidding as his servants, but the Son sits at God's right hand.

The author has next to nothing to say about what they do when they are **sent forth to serve,** but his basic point is simply that all of them, without exception, whatever their ranks and orders (he mentions none), are servants running and not rulers sitting. However numerous may be the hosts and armies of angels filling the heavens, **salvation** depends on the one Son enthroned at God's right hand. Angels are subordinate and simply **serve for the sake of those who are to obtain salvation,** not from themselves but at the hands of another.

In breathing that word **salvation,** the author has opened up the topic of the next paragraph.

First Exhortation: Pay Closer Attention! (2:1-4)

By introducing his new paragraph with the word **therefore,** our author signals that he is about to draw a conclusion from the preceding. In solemn declaration (1:1-4) and poetic anthology (1:5-14) he has both stated and argued the superiority of God's speech in the Son over all his former speaking. Along the way he has contrasted

1. the **fathers** and **us**
2. days **of old** and **these last days**
3. multiplicity and oneness
4. **prophets** and **Son**
5. **angels** and **Son**
6. perishing and abiding
7. serving and sitting

Here in 2:1-4 he offers yet another contrast: **the message declared by angels** and **salvation declared by the Lord.**

2:1—The author's language is that of the courts: **valid, transgression, disobedience, just, retribution, attested, bore witness.** His appeal to his readers is not framed in doctrinal terms. He does not plead that they avoid some heresy or continue to adhere to orthodox views. He does not urge, for example, the divinity or messiahship of Jesus. Throughout his work his aim is consistently practical—but good and wise practice is of course bolstered by intricate scriptural interpretation and argument.

This paragraph is the first in a series of great admonitions in this book which is, as a whole, a "word of exhortation" (13:22).

Since his foregoing declarations and exhibits are inescapably true, the common coin of Christian conviction, the only logical conclusion, says the author, is that **we must pay the closer attention to what we have heard.**

The author appeals to a tradition of preaching and teaching, to a word known and shared in the community, the proclamation on which the congregation is founded and grounded. It is a known quantity, and it must be grasped and held in faith (8:2; 1 Thess. 2:13; Rom. 10:14-17).

The author reckons with the dread possibility that his readers may not simply **drift away** aimlessly but may be swept away powerfully by terrible currents (Prov. 3:21; 2 Peter 3:17)[14] and so lose not only a teaching, but **salvation** itself (1:14; 2:3).

2:2—This verse offers further grounds for taking the appeal with utmost seriousness. **The message** *(logos)* **declared by angels** functioning as mediators of God's will at Mount Sinai (12:18)[15] was not simply the Ten Commandments, but the entirety of the first covenant, especially as it was concretized in the sacrificial and cultic system. Law and Levitical priesthood are practically synonymous in Hebrews (cf. 7:1—10:18).

Even though it was not spoken directly by God but was delivered by angelic intermediaries, that ancient word was in force, **valid,**[16] and binding upon the people. Proof of that is shown in the fact that law-breaking of any kind, active **transgression** or lazy **disobedience,** met its proper and **just retribution** (3:2; 10:35; 11:26).

2:3—If a preliminary word brings responsibility, how much greater is the responsibility attending an ultimate message? And if disobedience toward the passing word had dire consequences, how much more severe will be the criticism imposed upon a careless attitude toward the final word? Our author is arguing from the lesser to the greater (see also 9:13-14; 10:28-29; 12:9, 25; cf. 3:3; 12:18-24).

How shall we escape God's judgment **if we neglect**[17] not just a preliminary word, but the eternal blessing of the new covenant here described as **such a great salvation?** How shall we come clean of guilt and sin, and how can we hope to enter the presence of God and approach his throne of grace, if we adopt an uncaring attitude in the face of such **salvation?**

We do not see that **salvation** with our physical eyes or grasp it with physical hands. Everything physical and tangible is earthly and transient. Salvation is a transcendent, eternal reality, kept in heaven, ready to be revealed.

The greatness of **salvation** is shown in the fact that it burst upon the human scene here below in and through **the Lord** himself. His whole being and doing was God's ultimate utterance to us (1:2). The phenomenon of Jesus in its entirety is portrayed as a word, God's vital speech into his world (cf. John 1:1-18; 5:25, 39; 6:68). Peter in the house of Cornelius spoke of salvation as the word God sent to Israel, proclaiming good news of peace in Jesus Christ (Acts 10:36). That definition is appropriate also here.

Declared at first by the Lord, salvation was then proclaimed and **attested to us** (the second generation of Christians) by those (first generation Christians) **who heard him** (cf. 13:7, 17). The author counts himself, along with his readers, as disciples at second hand, something Paul would never have done (Gal. 1:10-17; 1 Cor. 9:1; 15:8).

2:4—Those earliest witnesses testified to salvation, and the power of their word is not at all diluted as it passes from one generation to the next. God himself bore witness 1) **by signs and wonders and various miracles** and 2) **by gifts of the Holy Spirit distributed according to his will** (Acts 2:22, 43; Gal. 3:5; 1 Thess. 1:5). The truth and trustworthiness of the message of salvation is vouched for by witnesses both human (Chap. 11) and divine.[18]

He Became Pioneer of Salvation and Merciful High Priest (2:5-18)

It was not so difficult for the author to gather his bouquet of passages and display the glorious superiority of the first-born Son over the angels. Nor was it so hard for his readers to nod their agreement. Scripture taught it, and both their experience and their creeds confirmed it. They were inclined to favor the notion of an exalted Savior, seated upon an eternal and unshakeable throne, holding sway forever.

But what about his career on earth as a man of flesh and blood, opposed, distrusted, crucified? The author has just appealed to the earthly beginnings of salvation, to the events occurring *at first* (2:3). Were not these earthly experiences of lowliness and temporality weighty arguments against the Son's superiority? No angel was ever nailed to a tree!

The author now bends his talent to the task of demonstrating how it was precisely such tragic suffering that qualified the Son to be pioneer and author of salvation. Exactly such hard experience in the flesh was the indispensable presupposition of his perfection and exaltation.[19]

Not to Angels (2:5-9)

2:5—**Not to angels** could stand as title to the whole section beginning at 1:4, but the author has his eyes fixed especially on 1:13. **Not to angels** did God speak the words of Ps. 110:1 quoted there. He offers his own commentary on the words he has written thus far, calling them a meditation on **the world to come,** on unseen things above.

A new **world** is destined **to come.** Elsewhere the author calls it the coming age, the coming good things, or the coming city (6:5; 9:11; 10:1; 13:14). It is the new spiritual order above from which blessings already stream down into the lives of the faithful.

Angels have limited power in the governance of the present world. They are guardians of the present order. Only the Son is the heir of the future (1:2) and lord over it. He alone has it in his power to bestow the future, final blessings. He alone knows and leads the way to future salvation. **Not to angels** has **God subjected the world to come** but only to the Son, and it is his alone to grant. He has power to give access and open the door to it.

2:6-8a—The author quotes Psalm 8 with a slight variation. The psalm originally celebrated God's creation of **man** or **the son of man** (synonyms for humanity) as holding a position in the hierarchy of things only slightly lower than the angels.

The author of Hebrews, however, has taken "slightly lower" in a temporal sense to mean **for a little while lower.**[20]

The quotation continues exulting in humanity as **crowned with glory and honor.** The inclusion or omission at this point of the reading of some ancient texts—**and didst set him over the works of thy hands** (Ps. 8:6a)—does not materially affect the meaning of the passage. It looks like something added by an early Christian scribe with a passion for completeness. The thought has been expressed in Heb. 1:10 where Psalm 102 is quoted. The angels of course belong to **the works of thy hands,** and so the Son of man is set over them.

The quotation concludes by praising God for **putting everything in subjection under his feet,** that is, under the heel or control of humankind.

2:8b—Then the author begins his commentary, starting with the last phrase of the psalm. At an early date Christians found different ways to connect Jesus' enthronement at God's right hand (Ps. 110:1) with his placing his feet on all things as on a royal footstool, inscribed with the emblems of all nations and creatures (Ps. 8:6). Sometimes they regarded both enthronement and subjection as past and already accomplished (Eph. 1:20-22), and sometimes they viewed enthronement as past but total subjection of the powers as future (1 Cor. 15:25-27; Phil. 3:21).

Which pattern Hebrews follows is not crystal clear. What is plain is that the author is rummaging about for language to express both the believed presence and the felt absence of the Son's dominion. Hebrews speaks of what is at present seen and what remains unseen. The author asserts that **in putting everything in subjection to** man, God **left nothing outside his control.** All things really are under the feet of the Son. But he admits that **we do not yet see everything in subjection to him.**

Students of Hebrews have found two schemes in the work: one temporal and the other spatial. At times the author seems to think in temporal categories of what was in the past, what is the case now, and what will occur in the future. At other times the author seems to operate in spatial categories, contrasting appearance and reality, the earthly and the heavenly, things below and things above.

The author's personal outlook seems to be spatial. Nevertheless, he understands and respects the temporal habits of his readers, and he has at his disposal a body of traditions, both Jewish and Christian, many of which were cast in temporal terms. He respects those traditions but is at pains to interpret them in his own categories.

2:9—We do not see the Son's total dominion and control, **but we see Jesus.** In fact what is accessible to our senses is the lowliness of Jesus, and we see how fitting is the traditional use of Psalm 8.

The name **Jesus** has been in the minds of author and readers from the first, but it is peculiarly appropriate that the actual name of **Jesus** has been withheld until the author begins to speak about the earthly career of the Son. From here on it appears frequently when the author wants to fix attention on the Son's humanity (3:1; 6:20; 4-14; 7:22; 10:19; 12:2, 24; 13:12).

The psalm spoke originally of "only a little lower" or "just a few notches lower." But what the author has seen in Jesus makes him understand the psalm as meaning **lower for a little while** or "temporarily lower" **than the angels.**

What was **lower** about the Son was not just that he became a human being, but that he became a despised outcast who endured **the suffering of death,** just as in Phil. 2:6-11 his "emptiness" consisted in his taking the form of a servant obedient unto death, even death on a cross.

He, to whom all things are subject, himself became subject not only to the limits of space, time, and biology, but even to the assaults of the sharpness of death. That is what **we see,** and more. The author insists that we also see him crowned.

Good Friday and Easter are the central and unassailable facts of Jesus' career for the gospels, for Paul, for Revelation, and for all the rest of the New Testament. But those documents connect cross and resurrection in different ways.

The author of Hebrews writes that the Psalm speaks eloquently of Jesus. He was **crowned with glory and honor** not simply after death but **because of the suffering of death,** and not simply for himself but for all others.

The lowliness of Jesus may appear to be a dark riddle, but it served a splendid purpose in the plan of God. He died **so that by the grace of God he might taste death for every one.** That does not mean that he merely nibbled at it or pecked at it.[21] It means that he deeply experienced it in all its bitter sharpness. He took death into his own being and consumed it, and he did so on behalf of every human being. His death bears fruit in the lives of others.

God led the Son onto the path of suffering and gave him up, not coldly and unfeelingly, but as the working out and effectuating of a gracious design. God rules **by grace** (cf. 4:16; 12:15; 13:9, 25).

Perfect through Suffering (2:10-13)

2:10—It would be an oversimplification to say that Psalm 8 originally spoke of everyone, of human nature generally, and that Hebrews interpreted the psalm as meaning the one man Jesus alone. Instead of setting a distance between human beings in general and the one human being in particular, the author deliberately connects them.

God who created all things and all people had a design for saving them all. The cross may seem shocking, gruesome, repulsive, or merely enigmatic. But the author insists that **it was fitting,** in accord with God's design and appropriate to his own character.

Involved as God is in the lowliness of Jesus, he is still the Lord of creation, **for whom and by whom all things exist.** The almighty and eternal one stands behind the program enacted at the cross. In and through the humiliation of Jesus, God was enacting his plan for **bringing many sons to glory,** lifting them to the heights of his presence, to life before his throne. The way to joy led through a dark valley of shame (12:2).

Jesus had to travel that way first as **pioneer of their salvation.** He went as pathfinder and trailblazer, hacking an opening through impassable thickets all the way to the goal of salvation. Hence **pioneer** means both "forerunner" (6:20) and "cause" or "source" of salvation (5:9).[22] Out of his own crucified humanity there springs a new humankind (2 Cor. 5:17).

Suffering was imposed upon Jesus to make him **perfect.**[23] That does not mean that he became more moral and less sinful. His existence from the beginning to end was "without sinning," however much it resembled ours in every other respect (4:15).

Perfection in this context is a cultic or ritual term (cf. 5:9). It refers to qualifying ceremonies or acts of self-dedication to be completed as solemn preparation for admission into the presence of God. Hebrews says that his death is his ritual consecration by which he is qualified to enter the heavenly sanctuary as great high priest.

The gospel of John uses similar imagery as it speaks of Jesus' dedicating himself in the final hours of his earthly sojourn, consecrating himself that his people may be consecrated and sanctified (John 17:16-19). That dedication or consecration of his life at the cross is called a finishing or perfecting (John 19:30), and it is simultaneously the moment of his glorification or victory and deepest union with the Father (John 12:23; 13:31-32; 17:1-5).

The cross is the first rung on the ladder connecting earth and heaven. Jesus has by means of the cross ascended all the way up into the presence of God. He went that way not for himself alone but that he might lead up (cf. Heb. 13:20) many in his train to realms of light and glory.[24]

2:11—The members of the community have just been called **sons** (2:10). Hebrews began by asserting that not prophets and not even angels but only Jesus has obtained the great name of **Son.** He is **Son** of God and they are **sons** or children of God. So **he who sanctifies and those who are sanctified** are of God. They **have all one origin.** Before the foundation of the world, before angels sang together on the world's first morning, Jesus and humanity were solidly united in the mind and plan of God.

He **sanctifies.** This priestly metaphor signals that he cleanses people from their sin (1:3), makes them fit to step into the very presence of God, and qualifies them for access to the heavenly sanctuary. How he sanctifies and at what great price is hinted at in verse 14 but is spelled out and fully developed beginning in the middle of Chapter 9 (9:11-22; 10:10; 13:12).

Jesus' sonship is still unique, despite all the solidarity between himself and all the other sons and daughters. But they have **one origin** and one destiny, namely God who is source and goal of all that exists.

The unique status of Jesus is implied in the reference to shame. He was **not ashamed** to acknowledge his solidarity with all the other sons and **to call them brethren.**

On the first Easter morning the resurrected Jesus commanded the women to go to "my brethren" with news of his victory (Matt. 28:10; John 20:17). He had declared earlier in his ministry that all who heeded his word were his mother and brothers and sisters (Mark 3:34-35), and in a special sense he had identified with the outcasts as the least of his brothers and sisters (Matt. 25:40). But instead of referring to memories or traditions from the life of Jesus, the author quotes from three biblical passages.

2:12—The first quotation is from Psalm 22. The opening lines of the psalm were spoken by Jesus at Golgotha: "My God, my God, why hast thou forsaken me" (Mark 15:34). Here another phrase of the psalm is taken to be an utterance of Jesus. He is portrayed as proclaiming the name of God to his **brethren, in the midst of the congregation.** This looks like a reference to the work of Jesus in the days of his ministry, when he declared the message of salvation (2:3) by which he revealed the name or reality of God.

2:13—The second quotation is from Isa. 8:17. Having proclaimed God's name, Jesus, like so many prophets and proclaimers before him (11:32-38), ran into a wall of opposition and persecution. In his hour of trial, he **put his trust in** God, and so patiently endured (12:2), as we all must do.

The third of the quotations looks beyond ministry and crucifixion to exaltation. Death was not the last chapter in his life. He pressed through to glory, through the heavens, to the presence of God, bringing humanity with him. There he exulted, **Here am I, and the children God has given me!** (Isa. 8:18).

Of the Same Nature (2:14-18)

2:14—So Psalm 8 speaks of *man* and *the son of man* (Heb. 2:6), while Isaiah 8 talks of *children* of God who are *brethren* of Jesus (Heb. 2:12-13). The same words are used of him as of them: *son, man, children, brethren.* And it is no mere word game. They are bound in closest and most vital relationship.

They **share in flesh and blood** and they partake of **the same nature.** What they have in common, what he was not ashamed of sharing with them, is frailty and vulnerability. Genuine solidarity meant exposing himself to the assaults of all the powers hostile to humanity, including the sharpest of them all. He laid himself open to death.

In his own way our author is stressing what Paul asserts is another fashion. The Son in these last days is not like Adam in the first days. The Son did not seek to escape humanness and seize divine status above flesh and blood and all that human life entails. He bent low, with no trace of resentment or rebellion, even tasting death, and his death was the door to a fuller life for himself and for all the universe (Phil. 2:6-11; cf. Rom. 8:3).

Precisely by sharing in flesh and blood and by accepting mortality, he was able to win his victory. **Through death** he was able to **destroy him who has the power of death, that is, the devil** (cf. Wisd. of Sol. 2:24).

2:15—By his trusting and obedient death he has pulled the teeth out of Satan and is able to **deliver all those who through fear of death were subject to lifelong bondage.**

Death enslaves by filling people with a sense of inevitable and irretrievable loss and by moving them to grasp for things in a desperate effort to preserve their lives. All of that self-serving maneuvering is a devilish invention. But the Son has broken the grip of that Satanic and Adamitic pattern and the lock it has on people's lives.

The devil maintains his power on a diet of people's distrust of God. Where disobedience and disloyalty toward God flourish, there the devil is strong. Jesus took flesh and blood, and then he traveled the downward way of self-offering, not full of fear and dread at the prospect of death looming before him, but full of confidence toward God. He went toward the cross freely (12:2); his trust in the Creator defeated the destroyer.

Verse 16 is a kind of aside, a footnote or parenthesis, momentarily interrupting the flow of the argument.

2:16—He was incarnate for the sake of flesh and blood beings, made human in order to liberate humanity. Although the Son is far superior to the angels, he was made for a little while lower than the angels, precisely because **it is not with angels that he is concerned.** Actually the passage means more than be **concerned** with angels. The word means "help." Jesus has not entered the word to help angels or to rescue them. (Another word for help is used in v. 18).[25]

Angels have been mentioned repeatedly since 1:4, but fittingly this is the last reference to them until 12:22 and 13:2. The whole way and work of the Son had as its purpose the parceling out of blessings not to angelic beings but to **the descendants of Abraham.**

The naming of **Abraham** expresses what should be obvious, that humanity is not an abstraction and that becoming human involves entering a particular family with a particular history.

Abraham was the greatest of the patriarchs, bearer of the promise, model of faith (6:13-15; 7:1-10; 11:1-19). The author takes for granted the early Christian teaching that Abraham is the ancestor of all the faithful, Jews and Gentiles alike (Galatians 3; Romans 4).

The author resumes his train of thought, interrupted by verse 16.

2:17—In order for Jesus to deliver the descendants of Abraham, **he had to be made like his brethren in every respect. It had to be.** It was fitting and appropriate in relation to God's grand design (2:10). Necessity was laid upon him by the logic of God's purpose.

He became **like his brethren** point for point, except that he never sinned (4:15). But in taking flesh he became as vulnerable, as open to temptation and to death as they are, and that was precisely the reason for it all.

It has already been stated that his sufferings in the flesh qualified him to become the pioneer (2:10). The word *qualify* or *perfect* implies a priestly preparation, but the notion of priesthood is now made explicit for the first time. He became human and opened himself to suffering, **so that he might become a merciful and faithful high priest.**

Every nation has had a sufficient supply of unfaithful priests, impious, self-serving officeholders and functionaries. Israel certainly knew from bitter experience the difference between faithful and unfaithful priests. Before the destruction of the temple and the cessation of sacrifice (A.D. 70), the Pharisees acted as watchdogs to ensure that priests acted at least in external conformity with the will of God as prescribed in law and tradition.

A genuine high priest must be qualified not only by Aaronic descent but also by personal piety (1 Sam. 2:35; 2 Macc. 3:1; 4:13). He must be **faithful,** and since the whole sacerdotal system is in the service of God's mercy and has mercy as its point, a genuine priest will be **merciful.**

While the author is very much in tune with tradition in his stress on faithfulness in 3:1—4:13, he is even more interested in effective mercy in his description of the Son as high priest in 4:14 onwards. But the two qualities complement one another. Because he has suffered, he is able to sympathize with humanity and, in service to them, is **merciful** (4:15). His sympathy does not stem from weakness on his part or from failure. He endured his temptations and sufferings without lapsing into distrust. He was **faithful,** perfectly steadfast. Because of his mercy and his fidelity he is a perfectly reliable and trustworthy priest.

Any priest is by definition a bridge figure, spanning the gap between God and humankind. The author pictures Jesus as standing before God or **in the service of God** on behalf of the whole human family. Israel had an intricate apparatus and detailed tradition regarding the functions of priests and of the high priest. The author of Hebrews has that ritual apparatus in mind, along with all the expectations bound up with sanctuary and priesthood. His imagination is especially captivated by the ritual of the great Day of Atonement (Leviticus 16), as the use of **expiation** in this context already reveals.

The theme of Jesus as high priest, here introduced for the first time, will undergo a mighty development in the following chapters. Here the author simply announces that all other mediators and systems have been superseded by the work of the Son in his incarnation, obedience, death, and exaltation. Not Michael or any other angel, not Abraham or any other patriarch, not Moses or any other prophet, but only the Son is the one final mediator and **high priest,** completely **merciful and faithful.** He has made **expiation for the sins of the people.** He has dealt definitively with them and has purified the people (1:3), qualifying them for access to God (4:16).

2:18—This high priest has himself **suffered and been tempted.** He was **tempted** not only after his baptism at the beginning (Mark 1:12-13 and parallels) and in Gethsemane at the end (Mark 14:32-42), but also in his exchange with Simon Peter in the middle (Mark 8:27-30). Gethsemane may be particularly in mind (Heb. 5:7), but the thought is wider. Every human experience of success and flattery as well as every encounter with spite and suffering can assault a person's trust in God and obedience toward God.

With this reference to the universal human experience of

being drawn away from reliance upon God, the author opens a window into his own thinking. His mind seems to be full of pictures of the sanctuary with its apparatus and furniture, its altar outside and curtain within, its progressively holier spaces, its grades of priests, and its days and times and seasons. Nevertheless, the author is not trying to promote any sacrifice but that of Good Friday, any sanctuary but that of the heavenly dwelling of God, any priesthood but the Son's.

This high priest is no mere abstraction or rarefied principle like wisdom, revelation, knowledge, or word, any more than he is an inhabitant of the world of spirits like an angel. He stands with his two feet on the ground in complete solidarity with his sisters and brothers. And therefore **he is able to help those who are tempted.**

The Christian church at an early date distinguished between lay people and priests. Then it began to elaborate grades and ranks of priests in imitation of Leviticus and Numbers, ignoring the logic of Hebrews (and the Acts and Galatians), binding people with legal and political cords to ritual requirements and dependence on officeholders.

The ramifications of the teaching about the high priesthood of the Son may have been difficult for the first readers of Hebrews also. The ability to grasp these ramifications perhaps formed part of the higher intelligence toward which the author almost despaired of leading them (5:11).

Chapter 2, verses 10-17 describe Jesus as pioneer (2:10), sanctifier (2:11), and high priest (2:17). As pioneer he traveled the most difficult path of all; as sanctifier he offered the most precious sacrifice of all; and now he is installed as most effective priest of all. He has brought many people to glory (2:10), sanctified them (2:11), destroyed the devil (2:14), delivered the enslaved (2:15), and removed their sins (2:17).

He was qualified (perfected) for such work only as human being, "brother" (2:11), and child of God with all the other children of God (2:13-14), standing with them in the depths of their trials and sufferings.

Therefore his humanity, with its lowliness, does not count against his being the mediator of salvation, and the readers' human lowliness should not discourage or dismay them. Trials and sufferings mean they are on the same path trod by the pioneer.

The section climaxes with talk of the Son as faithful priest, **able to help** the **tempted.** The Son's priesthood begins to be expounded explicitly in 4:14, but first the author pursues the themes of faithfulness and temptation in 3:1—4:13, as he recalls Israel's testing and rebellion.

■ Exposition: He Is Superior to Moses (3:1—4:10)

In 3:1—4:13 as a whole, the author deals with the theme of faithfulness (2:17). In 3:1-6 he compares Jesus and Moses, both of whom were, in their differing ways, faithful. Then in 3:7-19 he turns to rehearsing ways that Israel was unfaithful in the wilderness and suffered the consequences. Finally, in 4:1-13 he urges faithfulness upon his readers, that they may enter the rest that remains.

He Was Faithful Over God's House as Son (3:1-6)

Chapter 3 opens, as do the first two chapters, with a concise prose statement comparing Jesus and his work with great figures and events of the past. The author has announced the superiority of Jesus over the prophets and prophetic speech (1:1-4) and even over angels and angelic revelation (2:1-4). Now in Chapter 3 he sets Jesus down alongside the greatest human spokesman of them all, Moses.

Among all the many agents and prophets of God, Moses enjoyed a splendid preeminence as the single one to whom God deigned to speak mouth to mouth (Num. 12:1-8). Moses was praised in ancient Jewish circles as higher than the prophets and superior even to angels.

3:1—For the first time in this work the author addresses his readers directly. They are **holy brethren,** not merely of the author (3:12; 10:19; 13:22), but of Jesus himself (2:10).

In what sense are they **holy?** Christ has been named sanctifier (2:11), and removal of sin is his work (2:17; 1:3), and so, as people cleansed and benefited by that work, they are **holy** (6:10; 13:24).

He describes them as people **who share in a heavenly call.** Made by God and for God (2:10; cf. 1:2), they have God both as their source (2:11) and their goal (2:10). They were once called into being, and now they have experienced the new genesis of spiritual birth. God is calling and drawing them upward to life with himself along the same path trod by the Son (cf. Phil. 3:14; John 12:32).

They are summoned to **consider Jesus,** that is, to fasten their hearts and minds on him and so learn from him (10:24; 12:3; cf. Luke 12:24, 27; Acts 7:31-32; 11:6). To Jesus the author gives the strange title **apostle and high priest of our confession.** Was there a fixed formula or creed declaring that "Jesus is apostle and high priest"?

Apostle means authoritative spokesman and officially commissioned representative (what we would call a proxy), but in this passage **apostle** should probably be understood not as a separate title, but almost as an adjective modifying **high priest.** This latter is, after all, the chief title in the author's presentation of the work and service of the Son. So the sense of this phrase, which at first looks like a credal phrase with two independent titles, is that Jesus is the unique and final high priest, apostled or commissioned and sent by God (cf. John 9:7; 20:21).

Jesus and no other is the one we confess. He is the singular focus of our pledge of allegiance given at Baptism. The word translated as **confession** can mean either a fixed formula (a creed) or "our religion."[26]

3:2—Authorized and sent as high priest, Jesus was **faithful to him who appointed him.** To expound that faithfulness of Jesus, the author uses the Greek version of Num. 12:7, which speaks of the trusted place Moses held in God's house or among God's people.

According to Num. 12:6-8 (LXX) God reveals himself to ordinary prophets in visions or in dreams. But Moses is a priest-servant, faithful in the whole house of God, and God is more open with him, speaking to him mouth to mouth, clearly, and not in riddles or dark speech. Indeed, Moses beholds the glory of the Lord.

Jesus **was faithful, just as Moses also was faithful,** and yet Jesus has rightly been assigned **more glory than Moses.**

3:3—As great as Moses is—and to be greater than the prophets is to be great indeed—Jesus is greater still. Here the author offers one of his several proportional comparisons (cf. 1:4; 8:6). The glory of Jesus is to the glory of Moses as the honor of the builder is to that of his house.

The author could not and would not have used such a proportion if he thought Moses lacked glory. New Testament writers have several ways of comparing and contrasting Jesus and Moses. Sometimes Moses is praised and sometimes he is blamed (see Acts 3:22-23; 7:37; John 1:17; 6:31-32). Our author is and must be silent about such matters as Moses' disobedience in the wilderness (Num. 20:2-13) or his transient, fading glory (Exod. 34:33-35; 2 Cor. 3:7-11). It would have undermined his proportional comparison to point to any flaws in the character or work of Moses.

Nevertheless Jesus has the glory of being the **builder** of the **house,** that is, the founder of God's people, while Moses has honor as servant among God's people, who clearly existed before he did (11:25).

3:4—It was as the agent of God the Creator (1:2, 10) that Jesus established the house of God, and the author makes clear in an aside that he regards Jesus not as second God alongside the Father, but as the Father's image, effulgence, and agent.

3:5—The virtue of Moses consists in the fact that he was **faithful in all God's house as a servant,** and the service Moses performed was that of a prophet. His task was to **testify to the things that were to be spoken later** (cf. 2:3).

Praise and glory belong to Moses because he so clearly and faithfully testified in former times, in days of preparation, to things that have now been finally and fully articulated in these last days. Ultimate expression is the privilege of the Christ.

So Moses is here not legislator but prophet, and the content of his words is not a body of law but the promise of the coming of these last days and the advent of the fulfiller. It was a great revolution in human thought and religious history when the earliest Christian believers began not simply to discard Moses and the prophets, but to understand them as full of promise and to cherish the record of their deeds and words as a treasury of hope.

3:6—For the first time in Hebrews, Jesus is here designated by the title **Christ,** the Greek word for the Hebrew "Messiah," meaning God's anointed and appointed agent.

Of Moses it was said, following Num. 12:7, that he was faithful **in** God's house (vv. 2 and 5), but the **Christ was faithful** *over* **God's house.** And where Moses is praised as **servant** (v. 5), Jesus is extolled as God's **Son** and "heir" (1:2; 2:1-4).

House is one of the great New Testament images for the people of God. The word conjures up the picture of the people as a family or household (1 Peter 4:17) or, alternately, as temple, the place for the miraculous indwelling of the presence of God and of barrier-free access to him in all his astonishing truth and holiness. **House** pictures the people as God's family standing like priests in his presence, lifting holy hands in the rapture of worship, the intimacy of communion, the holiness of service (1 Cor. 3:16-17; 2 Cor. 6:16; Eph. 2:19-22; 1 Peter 2:5).[27]

The author insists that he and his readers **are his house if we hold fast our confidence and pride in our hope.** Whether they are God's house depends entirely on their relationship to the Son. They are God's own holy people, enjoying full and

free access to God, if only they **hold fast** [28] and remain steadfast in their **confidence and pride** [29] in the Christian hope.

Confidence is diametrically opposed to being burdened and
disqualified by guilt, despair, tiredness, or depression. It has
no traffic with a slavish attitude or timidity of spirit. What it
means is boldness in prayer, certainty of salvation, and confidence about every tomorrow, precisely because it is founded
on full and free access to God's own presence.

Pride means whatever it is a person is proud of and boasts
about. All will be well as long as the readers sustain their
bold boasting in their **hope** (Rom. 5:2).

And Christ himself is our **hope** (10:23; cf. Col. 1:27). The
congregation has been shaken, and there is danger that it will
fall back into the fear of death, into giving death and its
minions an importance not due them. The author urges them
to hold fast their confession of Jesus Christ as Son, as heir, as
pioneer, already sitting inside the heavenly sanctuary. He
has arrived at the goal of life beyond all death. Consider him!

3:7—4:13—The author has in 3:1-6 declared the **glory** of
Jesus and summoned his readers to **consider** him. In 3:7—
4:13 he builds on his opening declarations and develops a
chain of exhortations: **consider Jesus** (3:1), **do not harden
your hearts** (3:8), **take care** (3:12), **exhort one another** (3:13).
The author then begins to include himself in his admonitions.
Let us fear (4:1), *let us strive* (4:11; cf. 3:6, *if we hold fast*).

Psalm 95 (3:7-11)

Psalm 95:7-11, quoted at the head of the series of exhortations, controls the entire section from 3:7—4:13. It does more
than provide basic images (**today, voice, rebellion, rest**). In
the psalm (quoted in 3:7-11) the author discovers first of all a
severe warning for his hearers (3:12-19) and then also good
reason for strong hope (4:1-13).

Through the faith of hearts fixed on Jesus, the readers are
assured that they are God's place of dwelling, enjoying access
to him, but the author also recognizes the fearful possibility

59

of a lapse from faith. The congregation enjoys the privilege of having been addressed by the living God in Jesus and of being borne up as on wings of an eagle, but it has nonetheless been shaken and has grown weary. The people may indeed be murmuring like Israel in the wilderness, no longer confident that God is in their midst (Exod. 17:7).

Hardness of Heart Excluded Moses' Generation from God's Rest (3:7-19)

3:7—The psalm is not merely a piece of ancient history, a literary fossil out of Israel's past. It is what **the Holy Spirit says** even **today** to the Christian believers and partial believers.

3:8-9—The psalm recalls two incidents from Israel's past. At Rephidim the people had found fault with Moses and with God, not only complaining about the lack of water and calling into question the wisdom of the Exodus from Egypt, but even asking, "Is the Lord among us or not?" Moses renamed the place Massah, which means **testing** or proving, and Meribah, which means **rebellion** or quarreling (Exod. 17:1-7).

Later in the wilderness of Paran at Kadesh-barnea the 12 sent to spy out the promised land returned with stories of walled cities and giant inhabitants. On the very threshold of the promised land fear gripped the people and they murmured against Moses and Aaron, rejecting their leadership and rebelling against the Lord.

3:10-11—The Psalm summed up both incidents: **Your fathers put me to the test.** God was **provoked with that generation** and declared that he intended to strike the people of Israel with pestilence and disinherit them, but Moses interceded. The Lord listened to Moses and did not send a plague, but he **swore** in his **wrath** that all those who had in the wilderness tested his patience 10 times would **never enter his rest** (see Numbers 13–14).

3:12-19—In the Exodus and wilderness wanderings the people had seen God's glory, witnessed his deeds, and enjoyed his presence. But in spite of everything they hardened their hearts and distrusted his voice. Therefore they did not enter the promised rest.

Do Not Harden Your Hearts (3:12-19)

3:12—Having quoted the psalm with its capsule history of old rebellion, the author launches into his application, focusing first of all on terrible possibilities: **Take care, brethren, lest there be in any of you an evil, unbelieving heart.**

In 1 Cor. 10:1-13, a passage strongly reminiscent of Hebrews 3 and 4, Paul applied the experience of Israel directly to the Corinthian congregation. He recounted five deeds of God's grace and five actions of rebellion by Israel. Because they put God to the test, they suffered destruction. These, says Paul, are warnings for us, written for our instruction.

Faith and unbelief are dreadful opposites—one brimming with life, the other smelling of death. Faith means dwelling in the presence of *the living* and life-giving God (cf. 10:31), while unbelief means a lapse, a falling away, an apostasy from God, from the life we are designed to live, and from the persons we are created to be.

Unfaith is not just a passive quality or a neutral stance. It is an awful act of disobedience (4:6), a tantrum of disapproval and ingratitude toward God, akin to the Prodigal's severing of ties with his father (Luke 15:11-32).

3:13—As long as the psalms are spoken or intoned, as long as the present aeon known as **today** continues and night has not fallen on human history, we are summoned to *exhort* one another (13:22), lest any member of the house be **hardened** (vv. 8, 15) like Lot's wife with her wistful backward look to the city of alluring pleasures. Or, in the author's own rhetoric, to be **hardened** means to have a calloused heart, one that is **dull of hearing** (5:11), so that a person does not heed God's voice, but listens instead to the siren voice of the **deceitfulness of sin.**

The mutual encouraging to which the author calls the readers is to happen **every day,** perhaps in the daily gatherings of the congregation (10:25; cf. Acts 2:46).

3:14—Christians not only **share in a heavenly call** (3:1) but even **share in Christ.** In 1:9 the same word "sharers" is used of angels, but there it has been translated as "comrades."[30] Believers are the comrades or companions of Christ, sharing in all that he has attained. But the author is talking about a vital personal relationship. Nothing is automatic or mechanical. Everything depends on their holding **their first confidence firm to the end,** retaining their initial conviction from first to last, from its genesis to its perfection, from its first sprouting to its full flowering. It is not enough to make a good beginning. They are on a pilgrimage or in a race, and they must endure all the way to the goal.

3:15—By repeating the psalm verse, the author again reminds his readers that God is still addressing them **today** and that they must really **hear his voice** and **not harden** their **hearts** in a fresh episode of fatal **rebellion.**

3:16-19—The author drives home his interpretation of the psalm. God had overthrown all the king's horses and all the king's men, delivering his people with signs and wonders, leading them forth under Moses as pilgrims moving from bondage toward freedom, from the land of their past slave labors to the promised place of rest where they would enjoy his beneficent rule and dwell in his presence. But all God's efforts, so powerfully successful against the Egyptians, were undone by his own people. They escaped Egypt enjoying **the leadership of Moses.** But they were **rebellious.**

3:17-18—They were graced with miracles and sustenance for 40 years, but **provoked** God the whole time. Their history in the wilderness is summarized in the word **sinned.** They **were disobedient,** and to them he swore **that they should never enter his rest.**

3:19—God lavished his attentions upon his people, but their disobedience exercised a dreadful potency to frustrate the designs of the almighty. They were **not able to enter** the rest he himself had promised. Such is the terrible power of **unbelief** or faithlessness.

There Remains a Sabbath Rest for the People of God (4:1-10)

The exposition of Ps. 95:7-11 (quoted in 3:7-11) shifts now from severe warning (3:12-19) to urgent encouragement.

4:1—Bad news for the wilderness generation turns out to be good news for the readers. An entire generation perished in the wilderness, and whatever the following generation gained by entering the land under Joshua, it was clearly not the totality of the promised rest (cf. v. 8). Canaan was a mere shadow of the spiritual goal set before the people of God.

The ancient failure of the wilderness generation is taken to mean that **the promise of entering his rest remains.** Neither fulfilled nor cancelled, the **promise** is still valid. It remains in force as a possibility open to the readers and as more than a possibility. It is the manifest destiny of the readers. It is their goal and target, but they might yet fail to attain it.

Let us fear. The author summons to watchfulness, to a pondering of consequences, to a sharp listening, **lest any** of them be found to have fallen short, **to have failed to reach** the goal of entrance into rest, elsewhere called the failure to attain the goal of the grace of God (12:15).[31]

Hebrews urges treating **the promise** with utmost seriousness and as a matter of profoundest joy (see commentary on 10:23).

4:2—The promises of God are **good news: Good news came to us just as to them** (cf. 2:3-4). The Greek original might be overtranslated by saying, "And we have been evangelized just as they were."

But the author immediately continues with the sobering reminder that **the message which they heard did not benefit** those ancients, because it was not mingled or mixed with **faith** in those hearers. Some ancient manuscripts offer a different reading here as footnotes in the RSV show, but the point is clear enough: the good news yields benefits only where it encounters faith.

Faith is here named for the first time in Hebrews.[32] Other responses, both synonyms and antonyms of faith, have certainly been featured in the preceding paragraphs, especially in Chapter 3. There the author warned against hardness of heart, an evil and unbelieving heart, rebellion, and disobedience, while calling for perseverance in confidence and praising loyalty. The word **faith** now makes its initial appearance, and it is appropriate that it should happen here in the context of talk about the promise and of God as promiser. The discussion is reminiscent of Paul's treatment of word and faith in Rom. 10:14-21.

The author calls for **faith** most urgently because he recognizes that unfaith has the mysterious power to frustrate the almighty designs of God (cf. 3:19).

God has promised a rest, and he has in his wrath sworn that the generation of disobedience and unbelief **shall never enter my rest.** Who then will enter? **We who have believed enter that rest.** The last sentence contains a condition: We enter, provided that we have really come to faith and endure in faith. But it contains also a firm promise: The faithful are sure to enter that rest.

The author begins now to argue that the **rest** of Psalm 95 (3:7-11) means something far greater than the land of Canaan. He finds help in passages dealing with the Sabbath and in the Jewish tradition of mediation on the significance of the Sabbath rest of God.

The **rest** is not a completely future quantity. If it were, the ancients could hardly be faulted for failing to enter that which did not yet exist. So the author makes it clear that as soon as God had laid **the foundation of the world** (cf. 9:26), **his works were finished.** God began to rest, and so rest was available and ready to be entered.

4:4—Indifferent to the exact location (it is Gen. 2:2), the author quotes God's own word, **And God rested on the seventh day from all his works.** His rest has been a present and available reality from the beginning.

4:5—Then the author juxtaposes the reference to rest in Genesis with the mention of rest in Psalm 95. The one interprets the other. God's rest has been there from the beginning, and God had seriously invited people in the days of Moses to enter that rest.

4:6—But **because of disobedience** and unbelief (3:18-19), the ancient recipients of **the good news** (4:2) did not and could not enter. **Therefore it remains for some to enter it.** But if not Moses' generation, then who will enter and possess it? And if some **formerly** heard good news and so **formerly** had the opportunity to enter, when will such an opportunity recur?

4:7—The author finds his answers in the word **today,** spoken through David **so long afterward,** indeed many centuries after the Exodus and the failure of the people in the wilderness. The word **today** is full of promise. David himself did not receive the promise of which he spoke (11:32, 39), but he was a witness to it and to the power of faith.

4:8—**If Joshua had given rest,** the great and promised rest, to the people who entered Canaan, **God would not speak** through David in the Psalm so much **later of another day.**

4:9—**So then,** concludes our author, **there remains a sabbath rest for the people of God.** The word *people* is emphatic. Individuals saw the rest or had faith in the promise and endured in hope through persecution (Chap. 11). But, as a whole, the People in the time of Moses failed to grasp their opportunity. God's plan is not merely that a few isolated individual persons should enter his rest, but that a people should enter.

The author does not talk about another people or a different people, displacing the old people of God. He says simply that ancients failed and that God's rest awaits **the people of God. Today** the people are once again summoned and invited to enter.

Sabbath rest translates a single Greek word apparently coined by the author of Hebrews. It is rendered as "a rest like God's resting on the seventh day" by TEV. A different Greek word lies behind "rest" in all the references from Psalm 95.[33]

4:10—Our entering into rest means ceasing from our labors **as God did from his.** Our **labors** are of several kinds. They consist of the struggles induced by insult and maltreatment at the hands of a brutish world (10:32-34; 11:32-38). Part of our labor is to strive to enter that rest (4:11), to run the race (12:1), to lift up sagging limbs and strengthen weak knees (12:12). Our **labors** mean everything involved in the process of spiritual maturation and attaining to the goal of perfection (5:11—6:20). Beyond all the labors is rest, or as another first century writer put it, "It is for you that paradise is opened, the tree of life is planted, the age to come is prepared, plenty is provided, a city is built, rest is appointed" (4 Ezra 8:52).

■ Concluding Exhortation: Strive to Enter that Rest (4:11-13)

The argument concludes with an appeal (v. 11) and a warning (vv. 12-13).

4:11—With the tragic example of the wilderness generation before our eyes, **let us strive to enter that rest** and see to it **that no one fall** as they did because of unbelief and **disobedience.**

4:12-13—These verses may contain portions of a hymn or poem on **the word of God.** (Other hymns or poems have been discerned in 1:3-4; 5:8-10; 7:3; 7:26.) The language of these verses is more elevated, the structure more complex, and the thought more solemn than that of the context.

Certainly the language is densely packed and vividly metaphorical, and the closest parallels are in other poetic passages, especially Wisd. of Sol. 18:14-16 (cf. Ethiopic Enoch 9:5).

Interpreters may argue whether these verses are poetry, but no reader can fail to see that God's word, depicted primarily as promise in the foregoing, is here portrayed as the sharpest possible threat to the life of the disobedient.

4:12—Five adjectives qualify **the word of God.** The first two stand alone and unadorned: **living** and **active.** The other three are modified by additional words: **sharper, piercing, discerning.**

The word of God is neither idle nor idly spoken. Its lively vitality is demonstrated and felt in its ability to cut more sharply **than any two-edged sword,** any sacrificial knife or warrior's blade. It can even separate **soul** from **spirit** (the closely knit psychic and spiritual components of our inner life) and **joints from marrow** (growing together in the inner recesses of our physical frame). It can divide the indivisible. Then climactically the point is stated plainly. The word of God discerns **the thoughts and intentions of the heart.** There is no secret refuge where our plans or desires or the honest truth about our inner condition may remain inaccessible to the probing knowledge of God. Apostasy and failure to enter God's rest issue from an evil and unbelieving heart (3:12, cff. 3:10, 15). What is the condition of your heart?

4:13—Once again adjectives are the controlling words: **hidden, open, laid bare.** The idea of running from judgment is old and familiar. Prophets pictured people as fleeing from God, panic-stricken, crying out to the hills to cover them, seeking hiding places in clefts of the rock. But God will send hunters and fishers with their snares to drag them in (Isa. 2:10; Jer. 16:16-18).

Before God **no creature is hidden.** All of them are **open** or literally "naked." They are caught with no fig leaves, no excuses, no defenses. **Laid bare** is literally "with neck extended" and thus unprotected.[34] Hence the total picture of verse 13 is of a captive held firmly, body stripped, head thrown back with throat exposed to the executioner's sword—or it may be a picture of a sacrificial animal ready for the priest's knife.

The word of invitation and promise, when scorned, rebounds as an incisive instrument of judgment. To disregard it would mean unmitigated disaster, total loss, exclusion from life.

Elsewhere the word of promise functions either as a rock on which people build or as one over which they stumble (1 Peter 2:6-8). One thing it never is—a matter of mere indifference (cf. Mark 8:38; John 12:48; 1 Cor. 4:5).

All the secret convolutions of our hearts are open to **the eyes of him with whom we have to do,** the one to whom we must give account.

The Content and Function of 3:1—4:13

Chapter 3:1—4:13 has focused on the **rest**, on the **unbelief** which defeats God's plan to bestow his rest, and on **faith** which seizes and appropriates that promise **today**. This section appears to interrupt the author's train of thought. He had just introduced the theme of Jesus as high priest for the first time (2:17) and almost immediately broke off to compare Moses and Jesus and to speak not of priesthood, sacrifice, and sanctuary, but of God's rest.

However, the material in 3:1—4:13 is by no means unrelated to the sacerdotal and liturgical imagery which the author favors. In 3:1 Jesus is introduced as our high priest. In 3:5 Moses is described as "a servant." The underlying Greek word *(therapōn)* is used particularly of priestly service. Moses was widely regarded in ancient Judaism as a faithful priest superior to ministering angels sent forth to serve (1:14). Philo called Moses prophet and angel, king and priest.

Furthermore, the entire discussion of God's *rest* has shown that it is not an earthly space such as Canaan, but a transcendent reality. It is the equivalent of access to God's throne of grace and a synonym for the heavenly sanctuary.

Therefore 3:1—4:13 is not a mere interruption, and the transition from 4:13 to what follows is not as rough as is sometimes claimed.

Indeed, the last few verses on the critical function of God's word reach all the way back to the author's first sentences (1:1-4). Since the opening paragraph of his work, the author has been extolling the absolutely unique quality of the Word spoken in the Son. It is a pearl of incomparable worth and beauty, uttered not by prophets sent by God, not by angels ministering to God and to the people of God, not by Moses the faithful servant in the earthly house of God, but by one who is Son. That singular and final word ringing out *today* is God's promise of salvation (1:14; 2:3), rest (4:1), and access to his presence.

Let Us Hold Fast Our Confession! (4:14—10:31)

■ **Opening Exhortation: Let Us Hold Fast Our Confession of Jesus as Priest! (4:14-16)**

4:14—Here the author turns directly to the theme of the high priesthood of Jesus, which will occupy his attention all the way to 10:18.

Jesus is not a Moses leading people forth from an earthly Egypt to serve God at an earthly mountain (12:18-19), not an Aaron entering behind a tangible curtain in an earthly sanctuary, not a Joshua marching in the the vanguard of a procession into an earthly Canaan.

We have a great, an incomparable, **high priest who has passed** not merely over earthly boundaries and through an earthly veil but **through the heavens.** Jesus has been exalted far above whatever spheres ring the earth. He has passed through them all and is transcendent above the heavens (7:26; cf. Eph. 4:10). Since that is so, the author issues his call to his readers to **hold fast** their **confession** (3:1) or religion.

4:15—If verse 14 focuses on the Son's exaltation as Chapter 1 also does, verse 15 is reminiscent of Chapter 2 with its focus on the Son's humanity. He is exalted but not distant or indifferent. This **high priest** is characterized as having a unique capacity **to sympathize with our weaknesses** because he shared in flesh and blood and all the frailty of our human frame (2:14; cf. Mark 14:38). He suffered and he was tempted **in every respect as we are** (2:17-18), but he never yielded to sin. Our author pictures Jesus as emerging from a real agony of struggle unstained and unscathed.

4:16—Since we have such an exalted and compassionate priest, says the author, **Let us then with confidence,** in boldness born of faith and hope (3:6; 10:19), **draw near to the throne of grace.** The purpose of the drawing near is to **receive mercy** and to **find grace** and favor as timely **help** in any hour of **need.**

The earthly tabernacle had its mercy seat (9:5), the earthly representation of God's heavenly throne. God who is rich in mercy (Eph. 4:2) is Lord of the universe and sits enthroned in the heavenly sanctuary above. The Son has been crowned with glory and honor after tasting death by the grace of God for every one (2:9). **Throne of grace** means that grace is on the throne of the universe. Grace is invincible, unless we defeat grace by stiff-necked unbelief or soft lassitude.

Let us draw near. What is this drawing near? Is it the festal approach of priests through the curtain to the presence of God in search of atonement? Is it the solemn drawing near of subjects to their monarch in search of favors? Is it well summarized in the attitude of bold and active prayer? It includes these and more. It is a life of forward and upward movement toward God, a pilgrimage sustained by the grace of God who is himself the goal of pilgrimage.[35]

■ Opening Exposition: Jesus Is High Priest after the Order of Melchizedek (5:1-10)

5:1-10—Our author now proceeds to show how Jesus is qualified in terms of the two basic tests of any genuine high priest.

Appointed Priest by God (5:1-6)

5:1—In the first place, **every high priest** receives his office for one purpose: **to act on behalf of men**—other human beings just like himself. He is one of them (Num. 8:6), reaching out on their behalf toward God. His task is to bridge the gap between them and God, repairing their broken relationship with God by approaching God with appropriate **gifts and sacrifices for sins** (8:3; 9:9).

5:2—Human like those on whose behalf he serves and **himself beset with weakness** (4:15), however indignant he may be at the sight of human folly and disobedience, **he can deal**

70

gently with the ignorant and wayward. (He is not talking here of people who commit apostasy or sin presumptuously. See commentary on 3:12; 10:26.)

5:3—Because of his frailty, the ordinary priest must of necessity **offer sacrifice for his own sins as well as for those of the people.** Legislation for the Day of Atonement stipulates just such twofold sacrifices by the priests (Lev. 16:6-17; cf. Heb. 7:27). Unlike the ordinary high priest, Jesus did not sin, but he knows the human condition from the inside, and he is compassionate. Compassion is the first qualification of a true high priest.

5:4—The second qualification is divine appointment. **One does not take the honor** of being high priest **upon himself, but he is called by God.**

In the days just prior to and during New Testament times, Judaism was treated to the unwholesome spectacle of rival factions promoting their candidates for the high priesthood with threats and bribes. Because Roman governors controlled the priestly vestments and designated incumbents from among the candidates, the priesthood went to the highest bidder, the most powerful, or the least troublesome. Nevertheless, the principle was established already in the case of Aaron. The high priest is **called by God.**

5:5—Our author takes up these two qualifications in reverse order as he applies them to Jesus.

Christ did not exalt himself to the high priesthood. God gave him the glory and dignity of the office of high priest. To establish that claim the author quotes Ps. 2:7, which calls Jesus not "high priest" but "Son": **Thou art my Son, today I have begotten thee.**

This is one of our author's favorite texts (1:5), and with the whole of early Christianity he shares the tradition of the centrality of the unique sonship of Jesus.

It belongs to the author's genius and originality to have seen an intimate link between Son and high priest. The dignity of sonship entails the vocation of priesthood. The opening paragraph of Hebrews links the sonship of Jesus with the work of purification for sins (1:2-3). He has introduced this present section by confessing Jesus in one mouthful as great high priest and Son of God (4:14).

5:6—A second vital text for our author and for early Christianity is Psalm 110. He has quoted its opening verse in 1:13 to clinch his argument about the superiority of the Son over the angels. Completely without precedent is his seizing upon the fourth verse of the familiar psalm and seeing in it a revelation of the priestly dignity of Jesus: **Thou art a priest for ever, after the order of Melchizedek.**

The story of **Melchizedek** is recited in Chapter 7. All that needs to be noted here is that the author has found scriptural warrant for his assertion that Jesus did not grasp the priesthood but was appointed by God himself. By mentioning Melchizedek he has given notice that the priesthood of Jesus is certainly not like that of Levitical priests, exercised in earthly sanctuaries with animal sacrifices. But he is **priest** nevertheless—and **for ever.**

He Learned Obedience (5:7-10)

5:7—In 5:7-10 our author treats the second qualification: the ability to sympathize (cf. 5:1-3).

In Greek the passage is distinguished from its context by the heaping up of relative pronouns and participles and by doubling of expressions (prayers and supplications, cries and tears, offered and was heard). Both in Greek and in English the passage is moving and passionate. For these and other reasons interpreters have suspected that the author here made use of an early Christian hymn, and various attempts have been made to distinguish quoted material from the author's own editorial comments.

One reconstruction finds two strophes of three lines each, remnants of what was no doubt a longer hymn:

He offered up prayers and supplications
  with loud cries and tears
  to him who was able to save him from death.
He was heard for his godly fear
  being made perfect
  being designated by God a high priest.

The following phrases would then be the author's own comments: **in the days of his flesh, although he was a Son he learned obedience through what he suffered, he became the source of eternal salvation to all who obey him, after the order of Melchizedek.**[36]

If this reconstruction is correct, and it is of course hypothetical, it would mean (1) that the author is stressing the lowliness of Jesus in the days of his flesh (as he did in 2:5-18), (2) that he is applying to this unique **Son** a familiar Hellenistic notion that people have always **learned** through what they have **suffered** (hard experience is a school), and (3) that the author found his warrant for speaking of Jesus as priest or **high priest** not only in Ps. 110:4 but in an early Christian hymn.

5:7—The author has explicated the exaltation of Jesus to high priestly status by God (5:4-6). Here he is turning to the humanity and compassion of this unique priest.

In the days of his flesh, the time of his life here on earth, the Son was not involved in some sham or make-believe. He participated deeply and fully in the human condition. The author offers surprisingly few details of the earthly life of Jesus (cf. 13:12). In that respect he is very much like Paul and indeed all the New Testament letter writers. He has nothing about Bethlehem or Galilee, quotes no maxims or parables, reports none of Jesus' miracles or mighty works. But here the passion of Jesus and the events of Gethsemane leap from the page. It is Luke who describes Jesus' experience in Gethsemane as an "agony" or contest (Luke 22:44), and Hebrews uses a cognate in portraying Christian existence in its totality as an athletic contest or "race" (12:1).[37] Jesus

offered up prayers in Gethsemane with loud cries and tears
(Mark 14:34), struggling to determine whether his mission
could be accomplished even if God were to save him from
death (Mark 14:35-36).[38]

Not only on that occasion but continually he was heard for
his godly fear. The Gospels picture Jesus as praying before
he chose the Twelve, before he was transfigured, when the
70 returned with word of their mission, and on other occasions. But was he heard in Gethsemane? Not if being heard
requires being spared suffering and death. But his godly fear,
his piety, his trust (2:13), his devotion to the will of God, his
obedience (v. 8) rested upon the divine reality. God was
neither deaf nor absent. He was there, dependable, trustworthy, a sustaining and answering reality. And he has given
his response in the exaltation and glorification of Jesus (John
12:27-28). The God of peace has led Jesus up from death
(13:20), but he did not allow him a detour around death.

5:8—Although he was a Son, in spite of his absolutely unique
standing among all the children of God, in spite of his superiority to angels and Moses, he was not exempt from the severest
discipline of pain and suffering (12:5-11).

And he learned through what he suffered. Learned and suffered rhyme in the original, and the combination of terms
formed a familiar maxim just as "school of hard knocks" is a
phrase of more modern folk wisdom.[39]

Of course people learn all kinds of things at the hands of
suffering. Some learn bitterness, resentment, or self-pity. He
learned obedience. Doing the will of God was the whole purpose of his coming into the world (10:5-10), and Paul also
summarized the whole life of Jesus in the one word obedience
(Phil. 2:5-8). It was this obedience of Jesus both in easy circumstances and in painful which qualified him for high priesthood on behalf of all humanity. Even though the Son of God,
Jesus lived as our brother on earth. He experienced suffering
in his flesh, learned what obedience to God entails in a hostile
world, and so became a sympathetic high priest.

5:9—That suffering was a kind of qualifying test, a rigorous examination, a tough process of initiation by means of which he was **made perfect** (cf. 2:10). This is a pivotal notion in Hebrews, and it can be difficult, since it is used in an unfamiliar fashion. In Hebrews **perfect** does not mean what it ordinarily means among us. It is not part of the pair "sinful/perfect" (as in religious piety) or of that other pair "irregular/perfect" (as in geometry).

If we think of pairs of words, it belongs rather in the following sets: "uninitiated/perfected" and "immature/perfected." And since the word has in it the idea of reaching the goal or coming to an end, it is easy to see how it also bears connotations in Hebrews of death and dying.

Through his sufferings he was fully initiated into his dignity as high priest. Through the toils and agonies his earthly life ripened, blossomed, and achieved a shining maturity enabling this priest to serve as unexampled resource. Through the painful experience of death he was ushered into the heavenly sanctuary and took his seat at the right hand of God.

The closest parallel to this use of "perfection" elsewhere in the New Testament is the language of the gospel of John about Jesus' finishing or completing his work in and through his self-offering (John 17:4, 23; 19:28, 30; cf. 13:32; Phil. 3:12). Consecrated and initiated by suffering and death, in the full maturity of his moral authority, exalted to God's right hand, he became **the source of eternal salvation** (Isa. 45:17).

The main verbs in verses 8 and 9 are coordinated: "learned" and "became." Early Christians commonly connected Jesus' suffering and exaltation by defining the exaltation as the result or reward of the suffering. Hebrews says that the Son, adorned with the nimbus of his divinity and eternal power, took flesh and blood and so experienced suffering, and the Son who had so suffered became source of salvation.[40]

Elsewhere in Hebrews what is here called **eternal salvation** is designated "an eternal redemption" (9:12) or "the promised eternal inheritance" (9:15) bestowed on the basis of "the eter-

nal covenant" (13:20) established by his self-offering. It is
not an earthly or temporary reprieve of the sort offered by
politicians, armies, or doctors. It is **eternal**, belongs to a transcendent order, and is an unshakeable reality which will never
fade or pass away.

The one perfected through death is here called **the source**
as earlier he was designated "the pioneer" (2:10). He is pictured now no longer on the way, blazing the trail, but as
having attained the goal and functioning as **source**, fountain,
or cause of salvation. The author's great word for this activity
and status is **high priest.**

But first he makes it clear that this **source** benefits those **who
obey him.** Through his temptations and sufferings **he learned
obedience** (v. 8), and he rescues those who are linked to him
by bonds of obedience and loyalty, the practical expression
of their trust in the good news (4:2-3).

5:10—This **Son**, this **source**, has been **designated by God a
high priest. Designated** is here a parallel to "apostle" in 3:1.
He has been duly appointed and commissioned by God. He
is no pretender or upstart.

He is of course not a Levite, not of the house of Aaron
(5:4), but he is priest nonetheless. He stands in **the order of
Melchizedek.**

The contrast between Melchizedek and Aaron (5:6, 10; 6:20;
7:11, 17, 21) is stated as a difference in "order." It is not sufficient to think of the order of Melchizedek as new, rendering
old and obsolete the Aaronic or Levitical order. Actually
Melchizedek was priest at a chonologically earlier time than
Aaron or Levi, and so his priesthood is older. The difference
is that the Aaronic order is in the grip of transcience and
change and belongs to the material, temporal world. The order
of Melchizedek transcends this world and belongs to the eternal order. Whatever occurs in that eternal order bears the
stamp of unending effectiveness and permanent validity. Jesus'
priesthood is not Aaronic and earthly (temporal and temporary) but Melchizedekian (eternal and abidingly efficacious).

■ A Caution: Jesus' High Priesthood Is a Word Hard to Explain (5:11—6:20)

This is the theme of Jesus' high and final priesthood which will engage our author's energies in the heart of Hebrews (7:1—10:18), but before he settles down to that topic, he exhorts his readers in order to prepare them for the rigors of the exposition ahead.

5:11—6:20 interrupts the development of the theme of Christ's high priesthood, the chief topic of the entire section from 4:14—10:18. In 5:11—6:20 the author warns his readers that in order to make progress and grow to full maturity or perfection, they must break out of their sluggishness, their dullness of hearing, their intellectual and spiritual inertia, and grasp the "hard word" about Jesus presented in 7:1—10:18.

Milk and Solid Food (5:11-14)

5:11—About this, the matter of the high priesthood of Jesus in the manner of Melchizedek, the author has **much to say** (more even than he will say, 9:5), and he warns that it is **hard to explain.**[41] It stands in sharp contrast to "the elementary doctrines" mentioned below at 6:1.

They should by this time in their pilgrimage be prepared to handle the higher degree of difficulty involved in this teaching, but, instead of making progress, he fears that they **have become dull of hearing.** Literally they are "sluggish" (6:12), content to relax and settle down with what they are and what they have heard instead of pressing forward in their pilgrim's existence.[42]

5:12—They have lapsed into a state of arrested development. **By this time** in their Christian existence they **ought to be teachers,** instructing neophytes. Instead they are themselves like beginners working at the primary level.

They have never advanced beyond the **first principles of God's word.** [43] Below (6:1-2) he will specify the content of the Christian ABCs to which he here refers.

Using a familiar ancient maxim he tries to make his readers feel ashamed of their backwardness. They **need milk, not solid food.** They are like infants not ready even to be spoon-fed (cf. 1 Cor. 3:1-2).

5:13—They are babies or little children, happy with their milk and not interested in trying unfamiliar food. They have therefore remained inexperienced or **unskilled in the word of righteousness. Unskilled** means untried, inexperienced, ignorant, and therefore unable to endure.

So far the author has offered tantalizing synonyms for the word **which is hard to explain** (5:11). It is **solid food, the word of righteousness.** In substance, it is the material of 7:1—10:18 on the high priesthood of Jesus.[44]

And it is **for the mature. Mature** is closely related to "perfect" or "perfected" (2:10; 5:9).[45] Here the **mature** are described as **those who have their faculties** or powers **trained by practice to distinguish good from evil.** The author fears that his readers lack discriminating judgment in matters of morality and Christian teaching.

Let Us Go on to Maturity (6:1-8)

6:1-2—The call to **leave the elementary doctrine of Christ,** to abandon their infantile state and grow **to maturity,** leads to a brief description of the milk, the ABC's.[46] Those rudiments are organized in three pairs of phrases:

1. **repentance from dead works** and **faith toward God;**
2. **instruction about ablutions** and **the laying on of hands;**
3. **the resurrection of the dead** and **eternal judgment.**

These six items are connected in a complicated fashion: **Laying a foundation of repentance and of faith** occurs by means of **instruction about** two items dealing with Christian initiation—**ablutions and the laying on of hands**—and two items dealing with Christian expectation—**resurrection and judgment.**

Dead works (9:14) are deeds characteristic not of the way of life but of the way of death (Didache 1:1). They arise from death and lead to death. **Repentance** is a radical break from all such deeds and from the way of death itself. The unbelief or unfaith of the wilderness generation meant that they were unable to enter the promised rest of life with God and so were condemned to perish (3:18; 4:2).

Serious souls in every age have sought purification and cleansing, and in New Testament times Pharisees (Mark 7:3-4; cf. John 2:6), the Essenes of Qumran, John the Baptist (Mark 1:4-8), and the earliest Christian communities (Acts 2:38) practiced a variety of washings, including Baptism.

Instructions about ablutions explained the value of all these washings and their relationship to the great "washing" or "purification" accomplished by Jesus at the cross (1:3; 9:13-14; John 13:5-10).

Laying on of hands was a traditional way of expressing identity (and so of conferring membership, blessing, or health) and of transmitting authority (as in the case of ordaining elders and leaders). In the present context we should think of the use of the **laying on of hands** in connection with the initiation into the life of the community and sharing in the Spirit dwelling within the community.

The earliest Christian communities were vibrant with a lively sense of the truth of Jesus' **resurrection**, his sharing of his victory over the dark powers of the world with his people even now, and his imminent conquest of all evil in the great, final, and **eternal judgment** to come.

In a passage rehearsing the fundamentals of his proclamation, Paul spoke to the Thessalonians in terms similar to those used here, except that he does not refer to washings and laying on of hands. He wrote of the welcome he had among them, how they "turned to God from idols, to serve a living and true God, and to wait for his Son from heaven, whom he raised from the dead, Jesus who delivers us from the wrath to come" (1 Thess. 1:9-10).

Of course, the author shares these basics with his readers and regards them as the **foundation,** but he does not propose to rehearse this material. He intends to move forward and to carry his readers along with him to deeper water. He encourages them to make the effort of which he believes they are after all capable, in spite of the scolding he gave in 5:11-14. He wants them to advance with him.

6:3—This, this advancing, **we will do,** he says, **if God permits!**

6:4-6—For all his criticism of his readers, the author still expresses optimism by means of a sentence full of pessimism. He is so pessimistic about reclaiming those who fall away from faith and **commit apostasy** that he actually says **it is impossible to restore** them.

This is the first of four impossible things in Hebrews: It is impossible to restore those who commit apostasy; it is impossible that God should prove false (6:18); it is impossible that the blood of bulls and goats should remove sins (10:4); it is impossible to please God without faith (11:6). With such phrases the author expresses what he regards as obvious truisms.

The author has two ends in view. He wants to warn his readers about the awesome power of apostasy, of falling from faith into unbelief, which looms as a terrible possibility. In the second place, assuring them that he regards them not as unbelievers but as naive believers, he also wants to nudge and lead them along the path to mature faith. Of course, these two ends are closely related: he calls them forward because they are in danger of falling back. Only if they advance and contemplate all that Jesus is and does will they be able to endure in faith and live.

He assumes that they believe, that they do not need to have the foundation of their faith laid again, and that they can be stirred up to a state of readiness to hear the word "which is hard to explain" (5:11).

The author has already named six items as belonging to the basics. Now he describes conversion in a fourfold fashion.

He is not talking about four different events or four stages, but from four perspectives he describes what happened when people through **repentance** turned from old ways to faith.

1. They were **enlightened** (10:32), and that happened **once**, or better, "once and for all." Their eyes were opened or they moved from darkness to light, and they received the knowledge of the truth (10:26). "Enlightenment" was used of initiation into pagan mystery religions and into Christian faith and at an early date it became a synonym for Baptism in some parts of the church.

2. They have **tasted the heavenly gift**, experiencing eternal salvation and becoming open to the unseen world of God above. Some have seen a reference to the Eucharist here and a reference to Baptism in the preceding phrase. But the author is referring to the experience of the realities underlying both Eucharist and Baptism, and the phrasing of the passage owes less to sacramental uses than to Psalm 34, "Taste and see that the Lord is good" (cf. 1 Peter 2:3), and to the common religious vocabulary of the age.

3. They have **become partakers of the Holy Spirit** and share in divine and heavenly powers (2:4).

4. They have **tasted the goodness of the word of God and the powers of the age to come.** The author has just been talking about the basics as milk, and he would lead his readers to the more difficult word of righteousness as solid food (5:11-14). In the Spirit they have experienced **the powers of the age to come,** the energies of the higher world of God.

The author mingles metaphors of light and sight with those of food and tasting in an effort to express the rapturous delights of the experience of conversion, the passing from the wilderness of death to the land of the living.

6:6—Quite dramatically the author descends from lofty descriptions of turning to life and utters the harshest denunciation of how terrible it would be if the readers were to imitate Moses' generation. To taste and see God's goodness and then to **commit apostasy** (3:12; 10:26; 12:16-17) would amount to nothing less than to **crucify the Son of God on their own account.** It is not that they would be crucifying Jesus all over again, but that they would be joining the crucifiers and taking their stand with those who nailed him to the tree. Apostates heap **contempt** upon the death of Jesus, so that his blood can be of no avail to them (10:19-31). At the beginning of the second century, people of Bithynia who renounced Christianity proved to the governor Pliny the sincerity of their renunciation by uttering condemnations of Jesus. Pliny, in his report to the emperor, noted that he was satisfied, since no real Christian would do that.

Our author has employed such striking terms that generations of readers have found their attention riveted to the declaration that restoration is impossible for those who fall away. Rigorists found here confirmation of their idea that postbaptismal sin was fatal and that there could be no repentance for those who lapsed from faith in times of persecution. Those others who saw God's grace as the central and overwhelming reality of Christian existence regarded the doctrine of Hebrews as seriously flawed and resisted its inclusion in the canon.[47]

6:7-8—In 5:11-14 and 6:1 the author used the metaphor of the education of a child. Here the language of agriculture dominates. The words sound like Isaiah's song of the vineyard (5:1-7; cf. 55:10-11), John the Baptist's preaching (Matt. 3:10), or Jesus' parable of the seed and the sower (Mark 4:1-20). When the **land** has drunk the rain of heaven (Deut. 11:11) and yields **vegetation** and so is **useful,** it **receives a blessing from God.** But if the land produces nothing but thorns and thistles it **is worthless, near to being cursed** (Gen. 3:17-18; cf. Didache 5:1).

A tree which does not bear fruit is cut down; salt that has lost its savor is thrown out onto the road; ground which receives rainfall and is unyielding is fit only **to be burned** (cf. 10:26-27; 12:29). These are homely warnings for people who have tasted the goodness of the Lord and are in danger of falling back into an unfruitful unbelief.

Inherit the Promises (6:9-12)

6:9—His words have sharp teeth and are biting. The author knows it and begins to moderate his tone. Once again, he addresses his readers directly and with affection (cf. 3:1, 12). By calling them **beloved,** he indicates that this harshness derives from deep concern, and he also assures them that he is by no means pessimistic about their condition or destiny. He feels sure of **better things that belong to salvation.**

6:10—As encouragement, the author directs his readers to their own past and to the case of Abraham and bids them examine how God has worked in these two cases.

The writer has not forgotten and surely **God** will not forget their **work and the love** they have demonstrated and still do demonstrate **in serving the saints.** For example, they were steady and charitable in the risky circumstances of past persecution (10:32-34), performing exactly as the author would have all Christians live (13:1-6), and their lives are fruitful and not unproductive in the present.

Their deeds of love, done to **the saints,** fellow pilgrims, are counted as having been done **for his sake,** for the Lord's sake (cf. Matt. 25:31-46), and that means sincerely. The Lord will surely bless and not curse them (vv. 7-8). He is stern and disciplines his children (12:7-11), but he is **not unjust.** He will not **overlook** their service.

6:11—The author takes nothing away from his readers. He gives them their due. His purpose is that **each** should **show the same earnestness** in matters of **hope** as they have in the area of love. In this entire section our author has been summoning his readers to advance to maturity (6:1), and here he is focusing on their need to press on to **the full assurance,** the full scope or full development, of their **hope.**

Their love is admirable, but love without the undergirding of the hard word he is preparing to discuss is vulnerable. They need to hear that word with all the encouragement it entails for the forward and upward striving of Christian existence.

6:12—Once more the malady infecting the readers is diagnosed as their inclination to be **sluggish.** The same Greek word is translated in 5:11 as "dull" when the author expresses his fear that his readers have become "dull of hearing" and are not eagerly pressing to learn what lies beyond the rudiments. Not all will **inherit the promises** (4:1). It is obvious that whole generations have perished in the past without attaining the goal (Chap. 3-4). Those who have reached the promised rest or salvation did so through **faith and patience.** And the readers are urged to be their imitators (cf. 13:7).

The word **patience** can also be translated *tenacity*, which is a more descriptive word. A verbal form of the same word occurs in v. 15 where it is translated **having patiently endured.** Tenacity, however, sounds more active, less passive and resigned. The word family occurs only here in Hebrews.[48] Elsewhere the author uses other words for patience or endurance. But everywhere he is searching for terms adequate to his purpose of encouraging his readers to travel the long road through whatever difficulties with eyes lifted to the glorious goal, hearts buoyed up by the sure promises of God.

That tenacity, that steady advance forward and upward, that loyalty over the long haul, that determination to go the whole distance like a runner in a race is what our author means by faith. He will return to it after his exposition of the hard word in 7:1—10:18.

Steadfast Anchor of the Soul (6:13-20)

Chapter 11 is a full and memorable recitation of the tenacity with which ancient worthies clung to the promise. Here in Chapter 6 Abraham is mentioned just briefly as a prime example of enduring faith, and the accent falls even more on the divine action (promise) than on the human response (faith).

The emphasis on the divine basis of endurance and the naming of Abraham here, when his story will be recited in Chapter 11, seems surprising. Nevertheless 7:1—10:18 as a whole is intended as an advanced lesson in the heavenly basis for our faith and hope, and that section will begin with a meditation on Melchizedek, last mentioned in 5:10 just before this present piece of admonition and encouragement. Of course, the stories of Melchizedek and Abraham are intertwined.

6:13—Following the sacrifice of Isaac, the ultimate test of Abraham's faith (11:17-19), **God made a promise to Abraham.** The ancient Scriptures say **he swore by himself** (Gen. 22:16). When modern people swear, they may promise to tell the truth "so help me God" or "in God's name." Ancient Israelites took oaths with the words, "As the Lord lives" (1 Sam. 17:55), but God himself **had no one greater by whom to swear.**

6:14—This was the promise: **Surely I will bless you and multiply you** (Gen. 22:17, cf. 12:2-3).

6:15—That promise was threatened at first by Abraham and Sarah's childlessness and later by God's demand that Abraham sacrifice his only son, but in every circumstance Abraham proved tenaciously faithful. He had a son in his old age and received him back as though from the dead on Mount Moriah. It can be said of him that **he obtained the promise** (cf. 11:33) even though, of course, he did not possess it in all its fullness, but had to wait for "us" (11:40).

6:16—When God renewed his promise to Abraham after the offering of Isaac, he confirmed and elaborated it with an oath. In part this speaking of oaths paves the way for the reference to God's oath in connection with Melchizedek (7:20-21).

In all their disputes human beings guarantee the truthfulness of their words by means of **an oath,** and when they **swear,** they utter a name **greater than themselves** (cf. v. 13; Exod. 22:10).

6:17—God purposed to offer **to the heirs of the promise,** not only Abraham and his immediate family (11:9) but all those with whom God is concerned (2:16), solid proof of **the unchangeable character of his purpose.** In order to convince the heirs that he was reliable, that his plan was fixed and his will irrevocable, **he interposed** or intervened **with an oath.**

6:18—Hence there are **two unchangeable things,** two solid facts: 1) the word of promise and 2) the oath. God's word, alone and unadorned, is itself unshakeable and certian, for **it is impossible that God should prove false.** By swearing an oath, God has underscored the reliability of the word and has, as it were, doubled the solemnity and certainty of the promise.

What is his purpose in all this? The author employs a nautical metaphor. The readers are passengers on a storm battered vessel seeking a snug harbor (cf. Acts 27). Wind and wave threatened to sweep the ship away and cause it to break up with fearful loss of life (Heb. 2:1). The promise and the oath constitute **strong encouragement to seize the hope set before us,** as sailors jump to the command of a trusted captain issuing directions for the securing of a ship in troubled waters.

6:19-20—Hope, with eyes uplifted and hearts fixed upon the eternal order, is a spiritual anchor. The material world is in flux, and nothing within it can offer safe harbor for our lives. Hope is an anchor not dropped into the depths to grip the sand and rock of the floor of the sea but thrown forward into the future, thrown upward to catch on the immovable reality of heaven above. Hope is a **sure and steadfast anchor** cast into the heavenly sanctuary, mooring our lives to the unshakeable rock of **the inner shrine behind the curtain** or veil of the Holy of Holies (9:3-12). No storm can wreck lives so anchored.[49]

The nautical metaphor begins to yield to cultic language. Both pictures are vivid verbal elaborations of the fundamental Christian conviction that Jesus has been exalted as God's unique Son (1:1-4). We stand now on the threshold of the very heart of Hebrews (7:1—10:18). The sonship of Jesus will be expounded in sacerdotal terms, and that exposition is solid food that will promote the maturing of the readers, strengthen them on their way, and secure their lives as with a steady anchor.

The author has come to his great theme. Hope links them to the inner shrine where Jesus has gone as a forerunner or pioneer (2:10). That title in itself implies followers in his train and therefore already declares that he has gone ahead, not simply for the sake of his own advance in rank or power, but **on our behalf.** The Son has, for our sake and for our everlasting joy, become a **high priest for ever after the order of Melchizedek.**

■ Central Exposition: The High Priesthood of Jesus (7:1—10:18)

7:1—10:18 is the heart of Hebrews. This is the material the author had in mind when he wrote that he has "much to say which is hard to explain" (5:11). More advanced than the rudiments, more sublime than the basics, it is yet not esoteric doctrine. It is not reserved for a spiritual elite, a few initiates. It is meant for all, and indeed the author earnestly strives to communicate this higher knowledge so that all his readers may proceed to maturity.

High Priest Forever after the Order of Melchizedek (7:1-28)

Chapter 7 as a whole is a meditation on the mysterious figure of Melchizedek.[50] What the Old Testament has to say about Melchizedek is exceedingly brief but wondrously tantalizing. He receives a few lines in Gen. 14:18-20 and a single mention in Ps. 110:4. Spare as those references are, they set in motion a rich tradition, to which our author makes a unique contribution.

Priest for Ever (7:1-3)
The first three verses, a single complicated sentence in Greek, reveal our author's chief interest in the Melchizedek traditions: he is a priest **forever,** and the priesthood of Jesus is of the same sort (6:20; 7:3).

Our author has previously named Melchizedek in passing (5:6, 10) but now he settles down to a sustained commentary on Ps. 110:4, quoted in 6:20, which stands as a kind of text over his sermon on Melchizedek (Chap. 7). The author uses the Genesis narrative concerning Melchizedek as he contemplates the Psalm, approaching these materials in a manner like that of Philo, the first century Jewish philosopher.

7:1—In Greek the central assertion in this long sentence is clear: **This Melchizedek . . . continues a priest for ever.**

Melchizedek was **king of Salem** and **priest of the Most High God.** The author exhibits no interest whatsoever in identifying **Salem,** and it does not matter whether this city later became Jerusalem.

He went out and **met Abraham returning from the slaughter of the kings.** Cherdorlaomer and a coalition of petty kings from the north, raiding cities near the Jordan, had sacked Sodom and taken captives, including Abraham's nephew Lot. Abraham raised a force and pursued the marauders beyond Dan to the vicinity of Damascus, where he defeated them in a night attack. On his return with the captives and the booty he was greeted by the kings of Sodom and Salem. The latter was also a priest, and he brought offerings of bread and wine, and he **blessed** Abraham.

7:2-3—Thereupon **Abraham apportioned** to Melchizedek a tithe or **tenth part of everything.**

Having recited the basic story, our author begins his exposition. His own personal name and the name of his city show that Melchizedek is **king of righteousness** and **king of peace.** These interpretations occasion no surprise, but the author shows no interest in developing them. He obviously shares the biblical conviction that God's rule is a sovereignty of righteousness and peace and that God calls to righteous conduct, promising peace as the fruit of righteousness (1:8; 11:33; 12:11; 13:20). Peace and righteousness are the marks of the messianic age, but the author pursues none of this here.

His mind fastens on what the Genesis narrative does not say. The author takes it as significant that the Bible maintains a mysterious silence about the **father or mother or genealogy** of Melchizedek. He dares to say that Melchizedek lacks all these. In some uncanny way he is fatherless, motherless, without a genealogy.

Nothing is reported of his birth or death. From that it seems a great leap to conclude that he **has neither beginning of days nor end of life.** But the author of Hebrews was primed to note such omissions and draw such conclusions. In his meditations on the patriarchs, Philo uses the identical word "motherless" of Abraham's wife Sarah (cf. Gen. 20:12) and interprets that word to mean that she is not earthbound, not tied to the world of the senses, but is a spiritual being whose soul is advancing on its upward pilgrimage. Unlike the biblical record, Philo declares that Moses had no family except virtues and virtuous actions! God is his father and Wisdom is his mother. To be **without father or mother or genealogy** means to belong to a higher order of reality, not mired in the physical world which, though impressive, is temporal and passing away. To be a citizen of that superior order means, as our author says, to have **neither beginning nor end.** It means sharing in God's life.[51]

So Melchizedek in some small way resembles **the Son of God** just as the earthly tabernacle is a copy of the heavenly sanctuary. By pondering him carefully enough, lessons can be learned about **the Son.** The basic lesson is to be derived from Melchizedek's continuing as a **priest for ever.**

Abraham Gave a Tithe (7:4-10)

The focus shifts from things unsaid to things said and lights first of all on the matter of tithes and blessings. The stature of Melchizedek is glimpsed in the fact that even **Abraham,** who held the surpassing dignity of **patriarch,** spontaneously and enthusiastically **gave him a tithe of the spoils.**

That surprises, since the **commandment in the law** (Numbers 18) dictates a different practice. According to the law, **those descendents of Levi who receive priestly office,** namely men of the house of Aaron, have the right to **take tithes from the people,** that is, from their own people, **their brethren.** The

Levites enjoy exalted status among their people, but, privileged as they were, they were yet just one set of Abraham's descendants claiming tithes from another set. Levitical tithing was a case of Abraham honoring Abraham.

7:6—Not so with Melchizedek. He **has not their genealogy.** He is not one of the descendants of Abraham, not one of the brethren of the Levites. The author means not merely to declare that Melchizedek was no Hebrew, but to imply that he belongs mysteriously to a different and higher order of being altogether. He will explore that idea further in verse 8.

This non-Levite, this stranger named Melchizedek, **received tithes from Abraham and blessed him.**

7:7—What does that imply about the greatness of Melchizedek? It is axiomatic, says our author, that **the inferior is blessed by the superior.** So both in receiving tithes and in giving a blessing Melchizedek emerges as **superior** and the patriarch, for all his greatness, as **inferior.**

7:8—This verse ponders the phrase **continues for ever** (7:3; 6:20; Ps. 110:4) and takes the argument concerning the greatness of Melchizedek one step further.

The Levitical priests who receive **tithes** in accord with the law come and go. All those with their genealogy are **mortal men.** But the case of Melchizedek is completely different. Of him **it is testified that he lives.** He holds his priesthood unbroken and in perpetuity. That is evidence of singular greatness.

7:9-10—These two verses cap the paragraph with a third and final argument in support of Melchizedek's superiority. In a certain sense, argues our author, **Levi,** standing for all Levitical priests who ever lived and who in their superiority over their brethren ever received tithes, great as he was, **himself paid tithes** in this particular case. As the patriarch's descendant, **Levi was still in the loins of his ancestor when Melchizedek met him,** and in and **through Abraham** on that occasion **Levi who receives tithes paid tithes.**

A Change of Priesthood (7:11-19)

7:11—Without doubt the Levitical priesthood with its splendid sanctuary and impressive cult represented a magnificent religious tradition. But just as the promise of rest in Psalm 95 shows that Joshua did not give God's sabbath rest to the people (4:6-10), so the promise of another order of priesthood constitutes a poignant statement on the limitations of the Levitical order.

Perfection means arriving by a difficult path at the goal of fullness of life in the presence of God (see on 2:10; 5:9, 14: cf. 7:8-19). It means barrier-free access to God. Surely **perfection** was the point of Levitical institutions and of **the law** which accompanied the priesthood.

As the exposition proceeds it appears that the author has in view a tragic cycle consisting of divine commandments, human trespasses, priestly sacrifices making atonement; then the cycle begins all over again, endlessly repeating itself, never issuing in perfection. **If perfection had been attainable through the Levitical priesthood,** and the form of religious life which it symbolizes, the forward-looking psalm would not have promised the rise of **another priest after the order of Melchizedek.** The promise of such a priest reveals the inadequacy of the entire **order of Aaron.**

And if the priesthood is changed, **there is necessarily a change in the law as well.** Levitical priesthood and the old law belong to a single religious universe. They are integrally fused and bonded to form a single religious reality. The law was in force only as long as the priesthood under which it was received remained in force.

Our author shares the vision of God's people as "a chosen race, a royal priesthood, a holy nation" (1 Peter 2:9; Exod. 23:22). The official cadre of priests had vital functions and the law with all its commanding words ordered the lives and promoted the sanctity of the people. With the new priesthood has come a fresh ordering of God's relationship with his people through a new set of words.

On different grounds Paul also declares the law to be obsolete and no longer binding upon believers. It was never intended to be the way of justification and was merely a guardian or custodian until Christ came. Only he can bestow the Spirit and make alive (Gal. 2:15—3:29).

7:13—The psalm spoke not of a priest from the house of Levi and Aaron but of Jesus who **belonged to another tribe.** None of Jesus' ancestors **ever served at the altar.**

7:14—Much is made elsewhere in the New Testament of Jesus' connections with the royal line of David (Luke 2:4; Acts 13:22-23; Rom. 1:3). With David **our Lord was descended from Judah.** That is the house of kings (Luke 2:32-33), and our author here aptly designated Jesus as **our Lord** (1 Tim. 1:14; 2 Tim. 1:8; cf. Acts 2:36).

Judah supplied Israel with regents but **in connection with that tribe Moses said nothing about priests.**

For the moment it sounds almost as though the argument revolves around the legitimacy of rival claims to priesthood. Two candidates present themselves at the same altar before the same sanctuary to offer identical sacrifices. They differ only in ancestry. However, the ensuing paragraphs will exhibit the sweeping differences between these priests and priesthoods in every respect.

7:15—The old priesthood has been superseded and the old law has been set aside. All **this becomes even more evident** when we understand Psalm 110. Its shining promise has come true in the rise of **another priest,** radically different from all those of the house of Levi and Aaron. He has arisen (v. 11; Num. 24:17) **in the likeness of** (cf. 7:3) **Melchizedek and has become a priest,** not on the basis of fleshly and earthly qualifications, but on heavenly and spiritual grounds. For a development of this contrast see 9:6-14.

His priesthood is not legitimated by conformity to a **legal requirement concerning bodily descent,** proper genealogy, and correct blood lines. He holds a transcendent priesthood **by the power of an indestructible life.**

Genealogies with their sad refrains about begetting, living, and inevitably dying belong all too obviously to the temporal, transient order of coming to be and passing away. Levitical priests are clearly not marked **by the power of an indestructible life.** They are mortal, and it cannot be said of them that they are priests **for ever.** They are priests for a day or for a handful of years.

7:17—But the psalm says of our Lord **Thou art a priest for ever, after the order of Melchizedek.** His priesthood never ends and its efficacy never fades.

7:18—Priesthood and law, as has been said, are one bundle, and with the emergence of a new priesthood and the supersession of the old, the old law, or **former commandment is set aside.** That happened **because of its weakness and uselessness.** It was weak and useless in the sense that it **made nothing perfect** (cf. v. 11).

7:19—With the rise of a new priest and a new priesthood not only are traditional ordinances and institutions suddenly antiquated, but **a better hope is introduced.** Sin can at last be dealt with adequately (1:3). Perfection is possible under the new arrangement, and we are able to **draw near to God** (4:16), enjoying direct and lasting access.

Our **hope** is **better** precisely because it anchors our lives to the graceful realities of the inner shrine (6:18-19). Before that shrine and its liturgy are described (8:1ff.), the theme of the superiority of the new priest is carried to conclusion, as the author wrings from his text one final argument.

Not Without an Oath (7:20-25)

7:20-21—The installation of this priest into his office **was not without an oath** (cf. v. 28). Levites in former times **became priests** and **took their office without an oath.** Their priesthood rests on the simple and unadorned command of God (Exod. 28:1). However the narrative about God's dealings with Abraham (6:13-18) has argued the superiority of a divine word accompanied by a divine oath (cf. 3:11, 18), and Psalm 110 most explicitly and emphatically states that **this one was addressed with an oath,**

> "The Lord has sworn
> and will not change his mind,
> 'Thou art a priest for ever.' "

Our author views the psalm as God's solemn oath to Jesus. He who now sits at God's right hand will never pass away or be deposed but holds the priesthood forever.

7:22—Since the discussion up to this point has employed the rhetoric of priest, priesthood, law, and perfection, the conclusion might have been that we therefore have a better priest or priesthood, a new and better law, or a better hope of perfection.

Instead the word **covenant,** so important in the ensuing discussion, is introduced here for the first time, and the personal name **Jesus,** last encountered at the finale of Chapter 6 (6:20), also appears here.

In the original, verses 20-22 are a single long sentence climaxing emphatically in the word **Jesus.** He is the topic of this entire paragraph, but it is probably impossible to render the original Greek with a single clear English sentence. The best we can do is break up the paragraph into short sentences, concluding with the triumphant declaration: **Jesus is the surety of a better covenant.** He mediates it (8:6) and he is the guarantee of it.

7:23—The effectiveness of Jesus' singular priesthood so far surpasses that of Levitical priests that it is of a different order of magnitude altogether. Those **former priests were many in number,** and indeed had to be, because priests kept dying generation after passing generation. **They were prevented by death from continuing in office. Continuing** is a mark of the eternal and enduring world. However, men of the house of Levi, because of their mortality, were not able to abide or continue. They could serve only for a fleeting moment and were then inevitably succeeded by other mortal men.

7:24—Unlike all those priests without number, Jesus **holds his priesthood permanently.** It is not only nontransferable; it has an indestructible validity, since, as the psalm says, **he continues for ever.**

7:25—A priest is a sacred bridge between God and his people. This unique priest **is able for all time to save those who draw near to God** (v. 19) **through him.** Holding his priesthood "by the power of an indestructible life" (v. 16), called up from among the dead by the summons of the God of peace (13:20), **he always lives.** Death and transiency have no more power over him. He lives forever **to make intercession.**

The picture is not that of a begging Jesus, wringing his hands on bended knees before a reluctant Father, incessantly pleading our case before the heavenly throne. Rather he is one with God, the bright effulgence of God's glory (1:3), the ultimate gift of grace springing forth from the unfathomable mercy of God's own heart. That **he always lives to make intercession** means that he—not Michael or any other angel, not Moses or any other prophet, not Abraham or any other patriarch, not wisdom or law or logos—but only he is the eternally valid way, the everlasting link, the indestructible bridge. (See Rom. 8:31-38; 1 John 2:1; Acts 7:56.)

Perfect for Ever (7:26-28)

7:26—Here once again (cf. 1:2-4; 4:12-13; 5:7-10) the exalted vocabulary and rhapsodic style incline some interpreters to suspect the quotation of four lines from an early Christian hymn:

1. **fitting** for us was **such a high priest,**
2. **holy, blameless, unstained,**
3. **separated from sinners,**
4. **exalted above the heavens.**

Whether these lines formed part of a hymn, they do cap the chapter with rather different concepts from those employed in the immediately preceding paragraphs. The terms hearken farther back.

He is positively **holy,** because of his qualities of trust (2:13), fidelity (3:6), reverence (5:7), and obedience (5:8).

Negatively he is **blameless** and **unstained.**[52] He took flesh and was made like us in every respect, vulnerable to suffering and open to temptation as we are. But he was without sin (2:17; 4:15). Made for a little while lower than the angels (2:9), not ashamed to call those needing sanctification "brethren" (2:11-12), he was in fact maligned in the days of his flesh as friend of sinners and therefore sinner himself (Matt. 11:19; Luke 7:34).

But he is in truth no sinner at all. He is **separated from sinners,** as heaven is distant from earth. He is **exalted above the heavens** and lives in the power of a life at once indestructible and holy.

7:27—This high priest Jesus, holy and blameless as he is, is not constrained **like** those Levitical **high priests** of the house of Aaron **to offer sacrifices daily** and repeatedly, **first for his own sins** (cf. 5:2; 9:7; Lev. 4:3; 16:16) and then for **those of the people.**

Separated from the whole realm of sin and transiency, he offers a better sacrifice (9:12-14) with better results (1:3; 2:17). He dealt with sin **once for all when he offered up himself** (Mark 10:45; 14:22-24). The death of Jesus has of course been mentioned previously and so have the benefits of his priestly work. But now for the first time we hear that this priest offered **himself.** The full explication of this stupendous self-sacrifice will come in Chapter 9.

Once for all translates one of our author's favorite words (9:12; 10:10; cf. 9:26, 28; 10:2). The physical, visible, tangible world below is in the grip of flux, transiency, temporality, and is marked by confusion, multiplicity, and a dreary round of repetition. On the other hand, heaven and whatever belongs to heaven is constant, enduring, steady, unshakeable, and reliable. Whatever happens in heaven has no need of repetition but stands high and exalted above all mutability, temporality, and transiency.

This high priest, exalted above the heavens, has offered a sacrifice **once for all**. It is valid in heaven and therefore eternally effective.

7:28—The ancient **law appoints men in their weakness**, humans with all their baggage of sin and mortality, **as high priests**. That is simply the nature of the ancient system. But now there is something new. **The word of the oath** (Ps. 110:4) **came later than the law**. That implies a criticism upon the law, an acknowledgement of its deficiency (v. 11).

In expressing the astonishing newness of what God has done in Jesus, our author combines elements of Ps. 110:4 (**oath, for ever**) with the name derived from Ps. 2:7 (**Son**); the new **word** uttered by God with an **oath** (v. 20) **appoints a Son** (cf. 1:5) **who has been made perfect for ever.** The original has the final words in reverse order, and the emphasis falls on the last word: he is **for ever perfect.** That perfection has been noted before. Its basis has been stated (2:10; 5:9), and it has been argued that one system yields perfection and another does not (7:11, 19). The author is ready now to launch into his singular and moving exposition of Christ's "perfect" priesthood.

Minister in the Heavenly Sanctuary (8:1-13)

With the rise of a new priesthood, the old priesthood is superseded and the old law is set aside. A new order is introduced with the new priesthood, but it is not called a new law. Jesus is mediator of a new and better covenant (7:22).

The covenant mediated by Jesus is as much superior to the old as heaven is higher than the earth (8:1-6). Of course Scripture promised a new covenant, and the very fact of speaking of a second or new covenant implies that the first and former covenant was faulty and is now obsolete (8:7-13).

Minister in the True Tent (8:1-6)

8:1—The word has indeed been difficult to explain (5:11), and before proceeding the author wisely isolates the sum and substance out of the skein of intricacies comprising his argumentation.

Now the point in what we are saying about Melchizedekian priesthood **is this: we have such a high priest, one who is seated at the right hand of the throne of the Majesty in heaven.**

Jesus' victory over death and the devil was widely interpreted in the early church as his exaltation to God's right hand in fulfillment of Ps. 110:1 (see commentary on 1:3; also 12:2). It was the genius of our author to apply the fourth verse of the same psalm to the exalted Jesus and to expound his death and exaltation in liturgical and sacerdotal language.

8:2—He is now an officiant or **minister** [53] **in the sanctuary,** namely **the true tent** or tabernacle, pitched **not by man but by the Lord** himself (Exod. 33:7; Num. 24:6 LXX). How this **tent** is **true** or authentic and real and what it means that it was **set up by the Lord** God will begin to be explained in verse 5. But first comes a declaration on the liturgy performed by Jesus in the ideal sanctuary.

8:3—Just as **every high priest is appointed** with the expectation that he will **offer gifts and sacrifices,** so the same expectation attends also **this priest** Jesus. He too must have had **something to offer.**

This statement on the **something** he has to offer is not only brief but cryptic, and tantalizingly so, but explication will come in due course (9:6-14).

8:4—Here it suffices to note that he is not at work **on earth.** If he were here below **he would not be,** and would not need to be, **a priest at all.** Generation after swiftly passing generation, priests in numbers untold stand at earthly altars and repeatedly **offer gifts according to the** ancient and now antiquated **law** (7:18-19, 23). Whatever gift it is which Jesus offered as priest in the sanctuary of heaven, it is not the animal sacrifices of Levitical ritual enacted **on earth.**

That phrase **on earth** is as much a moral and spiritual term as it is a geographical term. To be earthly is to be inferior.

8:5—Levitical priests serve an earthly sanctuary which is a mere **copy and shadow,** an imitation or inferior reproduction (cf. 9:23) **of the heavenly sanctuary.** That is all it ever was designed to be. Grounding for this statement is found in **Scrip-ture. When Moses was about to erect the tent** or tabernacle, he received divine instruction through an oracle or in a dream (cf. 11:7; 12:25; Matt. 2:12). God himself instructed him: **See that you make everything according to the pattern** or model **which was shown you on the mountain** (Exod. 25:40).

Above this shadowy world of material things is the eternal order of being where God has set the true and archetypal sanctuary (cf. Wisd. of Sol. 9:8). Moses was granted a glimpse of that sparkling heavenly sanctuary by revelation on the mountain. The earthly sanctuary is a dim copy or faint imita-tion of God's heavenly dwelling place.

8:6—Levitical high priests ministered in the earthly sanc-tuary, the imitation, the copy. Jesus is minister in the original, real, eternal sanctuary, in the heavenly dwelling place itself. Furthermore his **ministry** or sacerdotal service **is as much more excellent than the old as the covenant he mediates is better.**

The language switches from the contrasts human/divine, earthly/heavenly, and copy/true of the preceding verses to more traditional talk of old/new. The former terminology be-trays a spatial mode of thought, while the latter is historical. The author's own fundamental outlook is spatial, but he easily accommodates the other view. He accepts traditional formula-tions gladly and either repeats them or recasts them into the spatial mode.

The covenant he ratifies and guarantees (7:22) is higher, superior, or **better, since it is enacted on better promises.** The author is about to specify what those promises are.

A New Covenant (8:7-13)

8:7—First he simply notes the obvious: **if that first covenant had been faultless** and had been able to offer perfection (7:11,

18-19), **there would have been no occasion,** no room or reason, **for a second.**

8:8—That God **finds fault** with the people of the first covenant and that he judges the first covenant to be weak or defective is clearly implied in the oracle of the new covenant in Jer. 31:31-34. And of course the oracle just as sharply defines what the superior or better promises are. The Lord himself promised, **I will establish a new covenant.**

8:9—It really will be fresh and **new** and not just a patchwork job of dusting off the old covenant and trying to make it work. The new will **not** be **like the covenant** which the Lord settled upon the people when he **took them by the hand to lead them out of the land of Egypt.** God's tenderness and care failed to achieve the desired effect, and the people **did not continue,** did not endure or abide in the **covenant.** Then as a terrible warning the oracle says that God ceased to care about them.

8:10—Yet the oracle is quoted not for its critiques but primarily for the better promises it contains. The Lord will inscribe his will not on tablets of stone but **on their hearts,** and he will deposit his law not in an ark of cedar but **into their minds.** People will know God inwardly, because he will reveal himself to them in the depths of their being. He will touch their conscience (9:9) and he will give knowledge of himself by granting free and full access to himself. For their part they will reciprocate by being his people indeed and by persevering in his presence (Exod. 6:7; Lev. 26:12; 2 Cor. 6:16).

8:11—Not only is the new covenant grounded in a deep, inward knowledge of God and expressive of intimate and enduring personal relations, but it is universal in its scope. No longer will prophets and teachers or anyone else need to rush about scolding or encouraging **every one his brother, saying, "Know the Lord."** The great promise is that **all shall know me, from the least of them to the greatest.**

Knowledge here, as so frequently in the Bible, means life open to life. God's life will be open to human life, and human life will move freely in harmony with his. That kind of knowledge will cover the earth as the waters cover the sea.

8:12—Thus far the newness of the new covenant has been spelled out in terms of inwardness and intimacy, accessibility and universality. However our author appears to have quoted the oracle at length, not for the sake of these relatively undeveloped motifs, but particularly for the sake of the bright promise embodied in the final verse of the prophetic utterance: **I will be merciful toward their iniquities, and I will remember their sins no more.**

This powerful promise of full, free, and final pardon is fundamental to all the rest. If the memory of sins can be obliterated once and for all, if the mountain of human iniquities can be cast into the depths of the sea and sink without a trace, if the deep stain can be wiped out and the awful burden lifted, not for a moment only but once and for all, then the covenant will indeed be new, and God and his people will realize a vital and intimate relationship heretofore unknown.

How such a covenant is mediated, by what sacrifices it is inaugurated, is the subject of the next two chapters.

Here our author caps the poetic oracle with a prose conclusion. The Lord God, merely **in speaking of a new covenant treats the first as obsolete** (cf. v. 7). The mere utterance of the word **new** sounded the death knell over the first covenant. It is marked as old, antiquated, outworn. **And what is becoming obsolete and growing old** is obviously in a process of decaying and is **ready to vanish away** altogether.

Christ Is the Mediator of a New Covenant (9:1-28)

In the very first sentence of his book our author simply announced without argument or elaboration that Jesus has dealt definitively with the sins of humankind (1:3; cf. 2:17). In Chapters 7 and 8, the beginning of the hard word or higher teaching, he has expounded his vision of Jesus as exalted high priest of a new and better covenant. Now he will make connections and fill in some blanks, explaining how it is that this high priest has abolished sin and gained for sinners unobstructed and enduring access to God.

An Earthly Sanctuary (9:1-5)

9:1—The first covenant has just been described as obsolete (Chap. 8), and the Levitical priesthood bound up with it has been subjected to sweeping criticism (Chap. 7). But that does not mean that we should henceforth ignore, let alone despise, that **first covenant.** Its **sanctuary** (9:1-5) and its **regulations for worship** (9:6-10), even though they are fleshly (9:10) or **earthly,** can still teach profound lessons, precisely because they are visible copies of the invisible originals.

The author will lead his readers from the copies to the originals, from a contemplation of earthly spaces and rituals to a meditation upon the heavenly liturgy. Heb. 9:1-10 deals directly with the **first covenant** and 9:11-20 with the new.

Our author comments not on the second temple, which stood in Jesus' day, the one rebuilt and made glorious by Herod the Great (see John 2:20), nor on the great temple of Solomon (1 Kings 8), but on the tabernacle of the most ancient period, the portable shrine of Israel's beginning, erected by Moses on a divine pattern revealed to him on the mountain (Exodus 25–30) immediately after the ratification of the covenant (Exodus 24). And he comments on that tabernacle as described in the Greek version of the Old Testament. Nevertheless the later sanctuaries, although they became steadily more elaborate and impressive structures, preserved the same basic ground plan and were the scene of the same rituals.

The epithet **earthly** defines the sanctuary and everything connected with it as belonging to the earth (8:4; Titus 2:12), to "this creation," as opposed to that which is "greater and more perfect" (v. 11), "eternal" (vv. 12, 14, 15) or "heavenly" (v. 23). It is a physical, tangible sanctuary erected on the earth by human hands. Yet this earthbound sanctuary is still at least a faint representation of the spiritual sanctuary above, and much can be learned from it.

9:2—Each of the two chief sections of the sanctuary is called a **tent.** In **the outer one** or Holy Place stood **the lampstand,** a single great menorah (Exod. 25:31-40), and a wooden **table** overlaid with gold serving as repository for **the bread of the Presence** (Exod. 25:23-30; Lev. 24:5-9).

These and the other furnishings were not merely ornamental or utilitarian. They were laden with meaning, since each piece in the earthly sanctuary mirrored some aspect of the heavenly dwelling place of God.

With its six horizontal branches and central vertical stem **the lampstand** of seven flower-shaped lights was a brilliant golden tree mirroring on earth the tree of life and the un-created Light associated with God's own place of habitation (Gen. 2:9; Rev. 22:2; cf. Exod. 3:2).

Twelve fresh loaves of fine flour, like the loaves set before honored guests, were arranged on the **table** each Sabbath as a thank offering and as a visible token of the communion between God and his people.

9:3—Beyond the first tent, **behind the second** or interior curtain, was another and even more sacred tented space called **the Holy of Holies,** a place of holiness to the nth degree.

9:4—Our author describes two pieces of sacred furniture as set within that inner sanctum: (1) **the golden altar of incense** and (2) **the ark of the covenant.** That description has its problems. All our sources are absolutely clear that only the high priest was permitted inside the Holy of Holies and he could enter only one day a year. Since incense was burned on the small altar twice each day, it had to be accessible on a daily basis to ordinary priests and so could not have stood in the inner sanctum.

It is impossible to say exactly what lies behind our author's description. The Greek version of Exodus, followed by our author, is vague on the precise location of **the altar of incense.** It says it was "before the veil that is by the ark of the testimony" (Exod. 30:6). The author may simply have drawn a wrong conclusion from the vague statement. Or he may have been influenced by the fact that the incense altar was closely associated with the ritual of the Day of Atonement and the annual entrance into the Holy of Holies. Blood was smeared on the horns of **the altar of incense** as well as on the mercy seat of the ark (Exod. 30:10), and burning incense was brought inside the veil on that day (Lev. 16:12-13).

The ark of the covenant was a wooden chest about 4 feet by 2½ feet by 2½ feet, covered with gold. Rings attached to its upper corners allowed poles to be inserted for easy transportation.

Into the **ark** Moses placed the second set of **the tablets of the covenant,** the stone slabs inscribed with the decalogue (Deut. 10:1-5). Our author describes the ark as sacred receptacle for two other treasures of the people's history: **a golden urn holding the manna** and **Aaron's rod.** The book of Exodus reports that, as a reminder of God's miraculous provision for his people, an urn of manna was kept in front of the ark (Exod. 16:31-36).

The restriction of priestly privileges to the house of Levi and the clan of Aaron, contested and opposed by murmuring in the wilderness (Numbers 16), was vindicated by a sign. Twelve wooden rods inscribed with the names of the twelve tribes were deposited in the tabernacle overnight. On the rod of the house of Levi was written the name of Aaron. In the morning it was discovered that **Aaron's rod** had put forth buds and produced blossoms and bore ripe almonds. So in addition to the manna, **Aaron's rod that budded** was kept in front of the ark as a sign that God had chosen Aaron's as the priestly family (Numbers 17).

As sacred repository of the decalogue, the official documents of God's covenant with his people, **the ark of the covenant** was the central symbol of the ancient faith. It was the earthly representation of the heavenly throne of grace (4:16). The ark was variously regarded as God's earthly throne or as his footstool. He placed the sole of his feet upon the sacred receptacle of the covenant documents in token that he himself had settled the covenant upon his people. The ark within the Holy of Holies was symbol of God's presence and reminder of his action on behalf of his people.

Above the ark **were the cherubim of glory.** Cherubim were fantastic creatures sculpted in gold facing one another with wings outstretched. They are **of glory** because they are unlike any earthly creature and belong to God, who is enthroned above them (1 Sam. 4:4; 2 Kings 19:15) or rides upon them as upon the wings of the wind and upon the clouds (Ps. 18:10-11). Set atop the ark, they are viewed as **overshadowing the mercy seat.** The gold cover of the ark bears the name **mercy seat** because of its special role in the solemnities of the Day of Atonement. Mercy is the focal point of the ancient ritual and of our author's own interest.

If Hebrews differs on where **the altar of incense** was located and on whether the rod and the manna were inside the ark or before it, the differences are negligible. Modern readers are interested in mathematical and scientific accuracy, but our author's interest in the sanctuary and its ritual is not antiquarian and historical, but passionately religious. All these ancient, traditional furnishings and regulations pertaining to the earthly sanctuary are a blurred but suggestive and extremely helpful representation of eternal realities above.

It is surprising to hear the author suddenly announce that he **cannot now speak in detail of these things.** He has been leading his readers along, apparently anxious to expound this hard word and solid food (5:11-12) about the earthly and heavenly liturgies.

What are the details he omits? He has said nothing about the number of lights on the lampstand or the number or arrangement of loaves set on the table, nor has he shown any interest in whether the bread was leavened or unleavened. He is silent about the vessels set on the table: plates and dishes for incense, flagons and bowls of libations. The Pentateuch is full of details about the sanctuary and its furnishings, the priests and their services, the calendar and festivals. What reader of Exodus or Leviticus or Numbers has not been numbed by the detail?

Or may the detail omitted be of another sort? Perhaps our author was not alone in finding spiritual meanings in the furniture and regulations of the earthly sanctuary. Might there have been a tradition of allegorical or spiritual interpretation current in his community? He might then be apologizing here for his single-minded devotion to one aspect of the earthly and heavenly liturgy and his silence about what, for his purposes, are extraneous details. He will speak allegorically a little later of the temple curtain (10:20),[54] but here he focuses unrelentingly on the ritual of the Day of Atonement.

Fleshly Regulations (9:6-10)

9:6—These items listed in 9:1-5 were the **preparations** or external arrangements for worship. Now comes the ritual.

Priests go continually into the outer tent, performing their ritual duties. Priests offer incense both morning and evening when they enter the sanctuary to dress and trim the lamps. And each sabbath priests eat the bread of the presence set in place as an offering to the Lord the week before, and they replace it with freshly baked loaves (Exod. 30:7-8; Lev. 24:1-9).

9:7—But into the second tent, the Holy of Holies, **only the high priest goes and he but once a year,** on the great Day of Atonement. And the high priest did not dare set foot behind the curtain and step into the inner sanctum **without taking blood.** He entered three or four times, taking a censer full of coals of fire and two handfuls of sweet incense and the blood of a bullock sacrificed as a sin offering **for himself** and for all the priests. And he takes the blood of a goat sacrificed for the unwitting sins or **errors of the people.**

He sprinkles the mercy seat with the **blood** of the bullock and the **blood** of the goat. That word **blood** echoes and re-echoes 12 times through this chapter and the next, as our author attempts to fathom the horror of sin, the terror of holiness, and the unfathomable mystery of the mercy of God.

9:8—By this, by the fact that access to the Holy of Holies was so severely restricted, **the Holy Spirit indicates that the way into the** true **sanctuary** of heaven, into God's own presence, **is not yet opened as long as the outer tent is still standing.**

Obviously, free and unimpeded access to God (perfection) was not granted by means of the first covenant and the Levitical priesthood. The strictures pertaining to entrance into the Holy of Holies and the narrowing of access to a single person only one day of the entire year are important elements in the lessons the author is intent on teaching. He says that these arrangements are **symbolic for the present age.**

9:9—But what is meant by **the present age?** Is it the equivalent of "this creation" (9:11), this transitory and temporal world? Or does it mean the new age inaugurated by the exaltation of Jesus?

If it is the former, then the parenthetical expression (**symbolic for the present age**) might be understood as follows: the Mosaic sanctuary and the worship there are just typical of this present age. The materiality of that cult is a parable or symbol of the materiality of this creation. It deals with externals and can make only an external, superficial, or temporary difference.

But perhaps **this present age** means the new time opened up by Jesus' exaltation to heaven. In that case the author might be saying that the old cult, for all its faults and limitations, is at least a faint echo of eternal verities, and the mind or heart is led upward by a contemplation even of the echo. The material cult is the best available in a material world, and that is not awfully good; but it stands as a parable and symbol of better and higher things. Indeed its very weaknesses demand a more potent ministry and sacrifice, and that is precisely what has now been established.

The **gifts and sacrifices offered** according to the Levitical **arrangement** are not able to reach the heart and realize the fresh and profound inwardness promised in Jeremiah's oracle (8:10). Animal sacrifices **cannot perfect the conscience of the**

107

worshiper, bring spirits to maturity, or usher people into God's presence. All those rules about **food and drink and various ablutions** are fleshly, outward, bearing only on the externals and belonging to this creation. They are **regulations for the body,** and they are provisional or temporary, **imposed** only **until the time of reformation,** that is, until the dawn of that new age when God sets all things right (cf. Acts 3:21). And yet all these earthly provisions are a mighty parable of spiritual movements in the heights of heaven and in the depths of the heart.

Securing an Eternal Redemption (9:11-14)

The introductory paragraph (9:11-14) of this new section (9:11-22) consists of two long sentences. The first (9:11-12) focuses on the action of Jesus as heavenly **high priest.** The second (9:13-14) carefully defines the last two words of the first sentence: **eternal redemption.**

9:11—The opening word **but** corresponds to the **now** of 9:1. They go together like this: "**Now** on the one hand the first covenant had a sanctuary and worship (9:1) . . . **but** on the other hand the new covenant has a greater sanctuary and a better liturgy."

Christ appeared. Hebrews, in spite of its insistence on the humanity and vulnerability of Jesus (2:5-18), is completely silent about Mary and Joseph, Bethlehem and Nazareth. Instead of saying he was born, it uses a word emphasizing his revelation or manifestation in the world.[55] He came on the scene as suddenly and mysteriously as Melchizedek did, **as a high priest of the good things that have come.**

Previously the author has spoken of "the world to come" (2:5), and he will speak of "the city which is to come" (13:14) and of a better country, namely a heavenly one (11:16). The good things God has in store for his people are to a large extent still future (to speak from a chronological perspective) or still laid up in heaven (to speak from a spatial perspective), and not yet granted fully in this time and this space. But some great benefits belonging to the world and city to come, to that heavenly country, are already mediated to his people by Christ the high priest. His people have already in this world had their eyes opened to heaven's light, have tasted the heavenly gift, have become partakers of the Holy Spirit, have experienced even here something of the powers of the coming age (6:5).

He became high priest when he passed **through the greater and more perfect tent,** one **not made with hands,** not conceived by any human architects and planners, not erected by human craftsmen and builders, **not of this creation,** not earthly, not material, not provisional, but true and eternal (8:2; Mark 14:58). He passed through all the heavenly spheres there are (2 Cor. 12:2), and he **entered into the Holy Place,** into the perfect sanctuary of heaven itself (9:24). He has made his entrance **once for all**—not twice daily, not annually, like Levitical priests—and he has dealt with sins **once for all,** and that means fully, finally, and forever.[56]

The RSV is misleading at this point. It pictures Levitical high priests entering the inner sanctum carrying **the blood of goats and calves,** which is unobjectionable, but then it proceeds to depict the crucified and resurrected Jesus striding into the sanctuary of heaven bearing vessels brimming with **his own blood.** The Greek text says nothing about **taking** or carrying. The author is commenting on the state or circumstances in which Levitical priests entered the earthly sanctuary and in which Jesus entered the heavenly sanctuary. How or in what state did they enter? A better translation would be: "not by means of **the blood of goats and calves** but by means of **his own blood.**" Or, he entered by virtue of his self-offering.[57]

Hebrews presents Jesus' death in two ways: (1) as the final moment of suffering and temptation at the end of the days of his flesh (5:7-8) and (2) as his entrance into the sanctuary of heaven as high priest. His death is simultaneously deepest humiliation and most sublime exaltation. His death is not just one more act of torture and persecution (11:35-38). The eye of faith sees his death as more, as his act of ministry in the sanctuary of heaven.

By virtue of his death, which is his offering of his life's blood and simultaneously his entrance into the true and eternal Holy of Holies, he has succeeded not merely in obtaining some small measure of relief or a temporary reprieve, but in **securing an eternal redemption.**

Because he is eternal Son of God (1:2, 5; 4:14), the selfless surrender of his life has **eternal** value and is effective once-for-all and forever, powerful above and so also here below.

Redemption (Luke 1:68; 2:38) means costly liberation. It pictures the freeing of captives or of slaves at a high price and joyous entering upon a glorious liberty dearly purchased (cf. Mark 10:45; 1 Peter 1:18; Titus 2:14).

9:11-14—Now the author proceeds to further definition of that **eternal redemption.**

Sin stains, defiles, and cuts a person off from the community of God's people and from communion with God himself. The first covenant had numerous provisions for dealing with sin, including but not confined to the powerful offerings of the Day of Atonement. On that day of course there was no **sprinkling of defiled persons with the blood of goats and bulls.** Sacrificial blood was sprinkled or smeared on the mercy seat and on the horns of the altar of incense (Leviticus 16). Ordinary sin offerings involved the sprinkling of blood before the veil of the inner sanctum and upon the horns of the altar of burnt offering and on the base of the latter (Leviticus 4).

This blood was not sprinkled *on* the people, but certainly was sprinkled *for* them. However, it is most important for understanding the passage to recognize that the author is thinking of sin as defilement and its removal as a cleansing.

He has already spoken of **various ablutions** in v. 10, and his main verbs in vv. 13 and 14 are **sanctifies** and **purifies.**

One of the chief ceremonies of the first covenant involving an actual **sprinkling of defiled persons** was the ritual of the red **heifer** (Numbers 19; M. Parah). A red **heifer** without blemish, upon which a yoke had never come, was slaughtered outside the camp. Some of the blood was sprinkled seven times toward the front of the sanctuary, but all the rest of the **heifer** was burned, not on the altar of burnt offering, but outside the camp (cf. 13:11-12) with cedar (durability), hyssop (cleansing power), and scarlet (blood red) cloth (cf. Lev. 14:4, 6).

The residue of ashes was carefully preserved by the priests. Whenever a person was defiled by contact with death (a corpse or a grave, for example), the ashes would be mixed with water and that person would be ritually sprinkled with a bunch of hyssop to remove the defilement and qualify the person to stand again within the assembly of the people.

Of course, water itself purifies, but in this case the water is vehicle for the real cleansing agent, the ashes of the red heifer, or the power of water to cleanse is amplified by the admixture of those potent ashes.

Once the sanctuary was established in Jerusalem, the red heifer was burned on a specially built altar on the Mount of Olives, connected to the Temple by a bridge thrown across the Kidron especially for the occasion. Red heifers were not burned weekly or even annually. The first was burned in the days of Moses, the second under Ezra, from that time till the destruction of the Temple in A.D. 70, only five or possibly seven were burned.[58]

Various arrangements under the first covenant have already been described as obsolete, weak, and powerless to make perfect (7:18-19; 8:13). **Sprinkling** ordained by that covenant merely **sanctifies for the purification of the flesh.** It has both cathartic and restorative power. It washes away ritual defilements and ceremonial impurities and it renders a person once more fit for community. But all those washings, including the most powerful, operate at the level of **the flesh.** They have validity on earth, in this transient age, in a human community bound by ancient but provisional traditions and rules.

9:14—Here our author offers another of his proportions (see commentary on 1:4). For all its shortcomings, he grants the old scheme a limited validity and effectiveness. But **how much more shall the blood of Christ . . . purify.**

It was required of the red heifer and of sacrificial animals that they be without any defect, such as lameness or blindness. So **Christ** himself was without blemish. But our author is thinking also here in terms of his phrase **how much more.** Christ was not simply without physical or fleshly defect. He was like us in every respect but without sin (4:15). Not just his limbs and bones and eyes but his soul and spirit and heart were **without blemish** (cf. 7:26).

Through the eternal Spirit he offered himself . . . to God. His sacrifice of himself was offered on earth but not as part of an earthly cult or ritual, not upon an earthly altar, and not for the sake of earthly or temporary benefits. His blood was not carried through a material tent to be smeared on a physical ark.

His offering was of a high and spiritual order. It is valid and effective in the realm of **the eternal Spirit.** His death outside the gates of Jerusalem in the first century of our era was an event on earth and in time, but above all it was an event once for all in the eternal order of heaven. It occurred in the transcendent heart of the universe and therefore its potency is universal in space and time, unrepeatable, and enduring.

Therefore his **blood** has the power to **purify** not just the flesh, but **your conscience** (cf. v. 9). **Flesh** (v. 13) and **conscience** (v. 14) are of course opposites. They are code words describing the basic components of the human being as bodily and spiritual, tangible and intangible, outer and inner (cf. 4:12). And it is precisely the innermost which must be reached and touched (7:10) if we are not merely to be purified from the pollution of contact with a human bone or a house in which a person has died, but if we are to be cleansed from **dead works** (see commentary on 6:1; cf. Mark 7:1-23) and turn to **the living God** with spiritual worship (cf. John 4:23-24).

When people stand in the presence of God with purity of heart, sanctified by the work of Christ, every barrier washed away, then will they have arrived at the maturity or perfection to which Christ has attained (2:10; 6:1; cf. 7:11, 19; 9:9).

Mediator of a New Covenant (9:15-22)

The death of Jesus is here interpreted as a necessary element in the ratification of the new covenant, first mentioned in 7:22. At this point, a review of our author's argument about the two covenants is in order.

In Chapter 7 he has explained that perfection was not attainable under the Levitical priesthood, which is transient and passing away. A better hope has been introduced by God himself when he declared with an oath that Jesus is priest forever. Thus he is the surety of a better covenant.

According to Chapter 8, Christ has attained to a ministry not in an earthly, transient sanctuary but in the true and heavenly tent. His ministry is better, as the covenant he mediates is better. The first covenant was criticized by God himself in the very act of promising a new covenant.

In Chapter 9 our author combines the motifs of new covenant and death, arguing that the death of Jesus is the indispensable basis of the new covenant. The gist of 9:1-14 is that the fleshly regulations of the first covenant dimly prefigure the eternally effective ministry of Christ. Levitical priests manipulated the blood of goats and bulls, but Christ entered the heavenly sanctuary at the moment when he offered himself without blemish to God.

So he is the mediator of a new covenant, settling an eternal inheritance upon the redeemed (9:15). That word *inheritance* triggers the thought that the same word translated as *covenant* also means "last will and testament," and for a moment our author switches from covenantal imagery to thinking of wills (9:16-17). When a person writes a will bequeathing an earthly inheritance to his heirs, absolutely nothing happens until he dies. The will simply does not take effect as long as he remains

113

alive. A last will and testament most clearly declares the necessity and potency of the death of Christ. In fact, the author continues (9:18), even the first covenant (now he switches back to his customary use of the word) was ratified with deaths (namely those of animals with their limited effects).

What is *better* (7:22; 8:6) about the new covenant has now been declared: it is founded not on a word only, but on a word uttered with an oath; it was ratified not by animal sacrifices handled by mortal priests in a sanctuary made with hands, but has its indispensable basis in the death of Christ who has entered the heavenly sanctuary as priest forever; the new covenant touches not the body only, but reaches the innermost heart and conscience; it bequeaths not temporary relief but an eternal benefit.

The death of Jesus, unlike animal sacrifices, was a free and willing offering of self in obedience and trust (10:1-13), and the covenant he ratified touches the mind and heart, dealing with sin and the seat of sin once for all (10:14-18). The blood of the new covenant speaks more graciously by far than the blood of Abel (12:24), and because his dying was the sacrifice inaugurating the new and eternal covenant, he lives and his people live in the power of indestructible and godly life (13:20-21).

9:15—The opening **therefore** (RSV) of this verse does not look back to the preceding but forward, and the verse might better be translated as follows: "For the following purpose **he is the mediator of a new covenant, so that those who are called may receive the promised eternal inheritance.**"

The readers belong to the company of **those who are called** (3:1; cf. 11:8). They have heard the voice of God calling them forward and upward out of their old entanglements towards **the promised eternal inheritance.** With Abraham and the patriarchs, they are numbered among "the heirs of the promise" (6:17). In the company of a vast throng, they are moving along the path toward the promised rest, the promised kingdom, the promised better country, the promised city.

Attaining the goal is by no means easy. Sins have always constituted a dread barrier and hindrance to progress (12:1). A terrible weight and burden of sin has accumulated ever since the inauguration of the first covenant. That covenant, taking sin and holiness with utter seriousness, was yet too weak to deal finally and fully with sin.

Nevertheless **a death has** now **occurred,** namely the eternally valid and effective sacrifice of Jesus' life (9:11-14), and precisely because his death is valid in heaven, eternally, and is not limited to a single moment in time, it reaches back and stretches forward. It is powerful enough to remove sins of the past **transgressions under the first covenant,** as well as sins in the present (see Rom. 3:25-26). All the accumulated debris of the past together with the offenses of the present are swept out of the way, and the people are able to move unencumbered and joyous on the upward path toward their **inheritance.**

Ancients, well attested by their faith, were blocked by the weakness of the first covenant from receiving the promise. But now the benefits of his death accrue also to them. The lightning of his sacrifice illumines their landscape as well as ours. And so, not apart from us but with us, they are perfected (11:39-40).

Such is the transcendent power of the **death** which **has occurred,** settling a **new covenant** upon God's people of ancient and of recent times.

9:16-17—The same word translated as **covenant** also means **will,** as in last will and testament, and the author plays on the double meaning (as Paul does in Gal. 3:15-18) in order to exhibit the vital importance of Jesus' death.[59]

Obviously the terms of a **will** do not go into effect until **the one who made it** dies. And the death **must be established.** If a person makes a will and then disappears without a trace, the courts demand that the corpse be produced or that a specified minimum number of years must elapse before that person can be pronounced legally dead. Then and only then can the dispositions declared in the will go into effect.

115

9:18—The connection between **death** and **will** is exactly the same as the connection between **death** and **the first covenant.** That **first covenant was not** settled upon the people and **ratified without blood,** that is, without a death.

9:19-20—After **Moses** had read to **the people every commandment of the law** out of the book of the covenant, and they had with one voice bound themselves to the words of the Lord, Moses took the blood of oxen and put it in basins. Half of the blood he threw against the altar, and when the people had bound themselves to the book of the covenant, he sprinkled them with the other half, and he said, "Behold the blood of the covenant which the Lord has made with you in accordance with all these words."

The preceding paragraph is a condensed version of Exodus 24:3-8. The author of Hebrews elaborates slightly when he speaks of **the blood of calves and goats with water and scarlet wool and hyssop.** Bunches of **hyssop** tied with **scarlet wool** were dipped in **blood** diluted with **water** for various sprinklings (see 9:13 and comments; cf. Lev. 14:4-6, 48-53; Exod. 12:22; Ps. 51:7).

Hyssop and **scarlet wool** may have been used in the case of the covenant-making ceremony also, even though Exodus 24 does not say so. And of course, where Exodus 24 says altar and people were sprinkled, Hebrews speaks of **the book itself and all the people** being **sprinkled** with blood.

But the point is clearly the same. Neither a human being's will nor even the first covenant, commanded by God, comes into force until a **death** occurs or **blood** is shed.

The imagery of covenant making and the very words about **blood of the covenant** are applied elsewhere in the New Testament to the Lord's Supper. On the night when he was betrayed, Jesus broke bread and poured wine, graphically signaling his death, and he said "This is my blood of the covenant" (Mark 14:25; 1 Cor. 11:25). But because Hebrews makes no use of the Passover, it also is silent on the connections between the new covenant and the Lord's Supper.

The Passover is primarily a festival celebrated, not by priests in the great sanctuary, but by the family in the privacy of the home. And our author concentrates on priestly activity in the inner sanctum of the sanctuary.

9:21—Our author continues his account of the necessity and use of death by saying that Moses at the time of the inauguration of the covenant **sprinkled with the blood both the tent and all the vessels used in worship.** Exodus mentions only oil in the dedication of the tent and all its furnishings and utensils (Exod. 40:9-11) and says nothing about blood at this point.

Josephus, a contemporary of our author, preserves a tradition that oil and blood together were used in Moses' consecration of the shrine. Our author knows of dedicating and cleansing at the inauguration of Israel's worship, and for him **blood** is the most powerful and effective cathartic agent there is.

9:22—He concludes his treatment of death and blood with a generalization: **Under the law** (the first covenant) **almost everything is purified with blood.** That little word **almost** leaves room for the fact that oil (Exodus 40), water (Leviticus 15) and fire (Num. 31:21-24) were also used as agents of cleansing or of dedicating. Nevertheless, after spoils of war were purified by fire they were also sprinkled with the "water of impurity," water mixed with ashes of the red heifer (Num. 31:23).

Our author then restates his generalization: **without the shedding of blood there is no forgiveness of sins.** The law of Moses does stipulate that a handful of flour might serve as a sin offering (Lev. 5:11-13), but that is clearly an exception established for people too poor to offer a goat, a lamb, or a pair of turtledoves—the ordinary offerings for sin.

Because blood contains the life or the vital principle, its consumption as a food was strictly forbidden. Blood is the most precious and potent of juices. It was granted the highest respect and was set apart because of its mysterious value and appointed by God as a means of expiation and atonement (Lev. 17:10-16).

Better Sacrifices (9:23-28)

9:23—Purifications on earth dimly mirror the superior purifications performed by Christ in the sanctuary of heaven itself. **It was necessary for the** earthly **copies of the heavenly things to be purified with these rites.**

Now of course the old sacrifices have been superseded by the blood of Christ. His death on Calvary's cross outside the gates of Jerusalem constitutes the **better sacrifices.** His offering is **better** because it is of infinite worth and has incomparable effects.

All this has been stated in preceding sections, but something strange emerges here. Our author declares that **the heavenly things**—sanctuary, furnishings, vessels, and utensils—had to be purified. Were they in some sense defiled and in need of cleansing? Some look for an answer to the book of Revelation and the casting out of Satan by Christ's death and resurrection (Rev. 12:1-12). Others suggest that God's people constitute the heavenly temple (3:2-6), and their consciences needed to be purified by the nobler sacrifices of Christ's self-offering (9:14).

Our author certainly draws a daring picture. He speaks as though the heavenly sanctuary was in existence but was not ready for use until **the better sacrifices** of Christ. Its heavenly benefits were only potential, a matter of promise, until that sanctuary above was dedicated and inaugurated with fitting rites and ceremonies. The death of Christ set in motion the use of that sanctuary and the flow of benefits from it.

The heavenly sanctuary existed even before the foundation of the world, the throne of grace stood within it from all eternity, and God has never been anything other than the God of peace (13:20), offering peace, grace, and mercy. But through the sacrifice of Christ, barriers on the human side are swept away, hearts are touched, consciences purified, and saints of times past and present are streaming to perfection.

9:24—As heavenly high priest the crucified and exalted **Christ has entered, not into a sanctuary made with hands,**

a mere **copy** or counterpart (1 Peter 3:21) **of the true one,** but he has entered **into heaven itself** (see commentary on 8:1-5; 9:6-10). **Heaven** is the true sanctuary.

Now at last he is there. The times of imperfection and of anticipation are over. **Now** he has entered to appear (cf. 9:11) there **in the presence of God,** before the face of God, not for his own sake but **on our behalf.**

That last phrase echoes throughout Hebrews. It is **on our behalf** that he tasted death (2:9), that he penetrated behind the curtain as our forerunner (6:20), that he makes intercession (7:25), that he has offered up himself once and for all (7:27; cf. 5:1; 9:7; 10:12).

9:25—Nor did he manifest himself in heaven **to offer himself repeatedly.** Repetition belongs to the imperfect world of matter here below, the world of coming to be and of growing old, the world of transitoriness and mutability, the world of birth and death (1:10-12).

Priests stand daily at altars, and **the high priest enters the Holy Place** (here our author means the Holiest Place, the inner sanctum itself) **yearly, with blood not his own.**

9:26—Christ's sacrifice is of a higher order. If he belonged to the same kind of priesthood as Aaron and the Levites, if his sacrifice had temporary effect and limited potency, if he were a sinful mortal offering a flawed sacrifice, **then he would have had to suffer repeatedly since the foundation of the world,** year in and year out. Then we would all still be caught in the prisonhouse of temporality and repetition, captives of mortality and mutability, inhabitants of a shadowy world, unable to break out into the light of glory streaming from the face of God, not able to enter the splendor of his presence.

But all that is contrary to fact. Christ has appeared once and for all (9:12; 1 Peter 3:18). The death of the eternal Son yields benefits unlimited in time and space, universal in scope, covering sins of the past as well as those of the present (9:15).

He was manifested **at the end of the age** (1:2; 1 Peter 1:20), in the fullness of time (Gal. 4:4), so that we now stand on

119

the border between the old and the new, the copy and the original, earth and heaven. And he opens the way from the one to the other.

He has appeared, he has been made manifest, simultaneously at the cross on earth and in the sanctuary of heaven (9:11-12), **to put away sin by the sacrifice of himself.** He has annulled and canceled sin utterly, opening the way to the throne of grace (4:16).

9:27-28—The argument of 9:26 continues in 10:1, but first comes an aside. The notion of Christ's appearing and dying **once** leads to the thought that humans also die **once.**

It is appointed. Moderns might say that it is simply in the nature of things. But it is God's design that human beings **die once,** and that is not quite the end, because after that comes judgment. Death is not just blessed relief from the weary round of repetitions or release from bodily woes, as was widely held in the ancient world. Death was the door to judgment, a springboard into the hands of the living God (10:31; 12:23).

However the faithful need not cringe before him who has the power of death, namely the devil, nor need they cower in fear before death itself (2:14-15). **Christ** has appeared in eternity before the face of God on our behalf. That same **Christ,** the one who has been **offered once to bear the sins of many** (2:10; 1 Peter 2:24; Isa. 53:12), he and no other **will appear a second time.** The second manifestation will not be for the purpose of repeating his sacrifice. That is excluded. He has already dealt a death blow to sin and he does not need to die again or in any other way add to what he has already accomplished. He will appear, but **not to deal with sin** again. Our author shares the early Christian view that Christ will manifest himself **to save those who are eagerly waiting for him.**

Christ Offered a Sacrifice for Sin and Sat at God's Right Hand (10:1-18)

After the interlude on human death and sure and certain judgment beyond death (9:27-28), the argument of 9:26 resumes. Christ's self-offering once and for all wrote "cancelled" across the entire sad accumulation of human sin.

The Blood of Bulls and Goats (10:1-4)

10:1—Shadow (8:5) is the first word of Chapter 10 in the Greek original, and it is therefore emphatic.[60] A **shadow** is all that **the law** contains **of the good things to come** (9:11), the blessings won by Christ.

The law, for our author, is primarily the whole network of instructions ordaining the Levitical priesthood and the cult (see 7:11-12). So he is summarizing what he has said especially in Chapters 8 and 9 when he writes that **the law** and the ministry of the earthly sanctuary contain **a shadow** and do not convey **the true form** or genuine substance of the spiritual benefits acquired on our behalf by Christ.

The law ordained repeated animal sacrifices, and it should be obvious **that the same sacrifices continually offered year after year** can never **make perfect** (7:11, 19) **those who draw near.** All the ancient ceremonies involving the manipulation of the blood of animals, however dutifully performed in painstaking accord with the law, proved to be weak and useless in bringing people to spiritual maturity or in winning for them full and free access to God.

The author notes a sad restlessness in the incessant and ceaseless repetition of the offerings. Repetition and restlessness are signs of earthly existence, imperfection, and incompleteness.

Our author's phrase, **If the worshipers had once been cleansed,** is parallel to his earlier notes. "If Joshua had given them rest" (4:8), and "If perfection had been attainable through the Levitical priesthood" (7:11). Joshua did not bestow the final rest, the priestly ceremonies did not yield perfection, and the blood of animals did not cleanse worshipers once and for all. And so sacrifices continue year by year.

If the worshipers had really **been cleansed** once and for all (John 13:10), **they would no longer have any consciousness of**

121

sin. The same Greek word lies behind **consciousness** and *conscience* (9:14). If their consciences were purified and their hearts transformed (8:10), sacrifice would have achieved its goal and could have ceased in a godly rest. On *flesh* and *conscience* as opposites see commentary on 9:13-14.

10:3-4—But the very fact that these sacrifices continue and are repeated is evidence of their ineffectiveness. What repeated sacrifices do is to act more as a poignant **reminder of sin** than as remover of sin.

The author concludes with a ringing declaration less argumentative or didactic than oracular, brimming with the simple clarity of the prophet: **It is impossible that the blood of bulls and goats should take away sins** (9:9, 13). See commentary on 6:4 for our author's list of four impossible things.

It requires something stronger than goat's blood to remove the deep stains on the human spirit and in the human heart. But our author utters his declaration not in a mood of pessimism, overwhelmed by the enormity of sin and the futility of repetitious ritual, but in a state of leaping exultation and high confidence.

To Do Thy Will (10:5-10)

10:5-7—**When Christ came into the world,** when he was for a little while made lower than the angels, when he partook of our nature and shared in flesh and blood (2:5-18), then Psalm 40 fit him so perfectly that our author presents the psalm as a piece of self-description in the very mouth of Jesus.

The Hebrew manuscripts of the psalm have the phrase "ears thou hast dug for me," but the Greek version of the Old Testament, followed by our author and his community, has the reading, **a body hast thou prepared for me** (Ps. 40:6). The sense is finally the same: God neither desires nor delights in **sacrifices and offerings.** What does he want? Ears that hear and obey, bodies that do his will. But it was marvelously convenient and suggestive that our author found the word **body** in his texts of the psalm. He pounced on it. And he represents Jesus himself as singing, **O God, . . . a body hast thou prepared for me.** And he dedicated himself to using that body to realize what all **burnt offerings and sin offerings** could never do.

10:8—The author attends to the contrast in the psalm. First it says that God has **neither desired nor taken pleasure in sacrifices and offerings,** even though **these are offered according to the law.** But as the psalm continues it announces a substitute or alternative: **Lo, I have come to do thy will.**

Read historically, the psalm declares that God takes greater delight in a person's wholehearted and ready obedience than in the costly range of sacrifices that person might offer. Obedience is better and is preferred before peace offerings, cereal offerings, burnt offerings, or sin offerings.

The psalm spoke of any person's life before God. But our author reads it as a statement about Jesus and indeed as an utterance of Jesus.

The first—the whole system of ritual and sacrifice—is abolished and swept away, not crankily or petulantly but **in order to establish the second,** in order to make room for the true and spiritual service of God (John 4:23-24), in a deep and inward resonance with the **will** of God (8:10).

10:10—**By that will** and design of God revealed in the psalm, Jesus came into the world, took the body prepared for him (10:5), exposed himself to all that bodies of flesh and blood are heir to, including temptation and suffering, and in that body he even tasted death (2:9-10). All this he did with neither grudging nor complaint. In it all he learned obedience (5:8), and he expressed obedience and filial trust (2:13). He endured it all as the voluntary and obedient **offering of the body.**

That joyful trust and spontaneous obedience lift his self-offering far above the level of the offering of dumb beasts, as far as heaven is above the earth. The result is that **we have been** consecrated or **sanctified** and cleansed through Jesus' offering of his body **once for all.**

Christ Sat Down (10:11-18)

10:11—Our author is now rapidly winding up his exposition of his word hard to explain, the solid food or word of righteousness (5:11-14). But before he finishes, he casts a final glance upon his basic text, Psalm 110 (cf. 1:13), and discovers there a word as yet unexploited. His comment is exceedingly brief and is tossed out as a kind of clincher. He simultaneously offers a fresh argument and reiterates his fundamental conviction about the finality of Christ's sacrifice. He fastens our attention on the word **sat,** and he expounds the significance of that sitting down in contrast to standing.

Every Levitical or Aaronic priest in the performance of his sacred duties in the earthly sanctuary **stands.** He **stands daily.** He **stands** at the altar of burnt offering, enters the Holy Place and **stands** at the altar of incense, **stands** at the menorah, **stands** at the table of the bread of the Presence. And when the high priest once a year penetrates behind the curtain, he **stands** as he censes the ark or sprinkles it with blood. Chairs were no part of the furniture of the sanctuary. Ancient iconography of Egyptian religion may picture the deity as seated, but the gods are always served by standing priests and devotees. Israel's sanctuary contained no statue of God. The prohibition against idolatry was strictly observed, and the ark of the covenant stood in solitary splendor within the Holy of Holies as the earthly throne or footstool of the invisible God (9:4). God was thus enthroned invisibly, and in his presence all stood.

The priests stood not simply as a mark of respect, however, but as a sign that they had an unfinished task. However **when Christ had offered for all time a single sacrifice for sins,** namely his own life in obedience to the Father, voluntarily given up at the cross outside the gates, then **he sat down.** His work was finished, complete, perfect (John 19:28-30).

He was himself perfected through his self-offering, qualified to enter the very presence of God in the heavenly sanctuary (2:10; 5:9; 7:28). Early in his composition our author said that, through his death, Jesus has been exalted to heaven and has taken his seat **at the right hand of God** (1:3, 13; 8:1). He is crowned with glory and honor, and everything has in principle been placed in subjection to him, although it is not yet apparent that nothing is outside his control (2:8-9). Here he expresses himself rather differently: Christ now waits for the inevitable concomitant to this enthronement, that **his enemies should be made a stool for his feet** (see commentary on 2:8).

Not a syllable is uttered to explain who **his enemies** might be. The phrase may simply be part of the royal and military imagery of the psalm, but it may also be employed by our author as an oblique warning to his readers to be wary lest they be numbered among those **enemies.** He will shortly turn from explanation to his final exhortation (10:19—13:25).

10:14—The chapter began with the declaration that the law, with its repeated, multiple offerings, can never make perfect those who draw near. The other shoe now drops: **By a single offering** Christ **has perfected for all time,** not for the next 12 months or for some even briefer span, **those who are sanctified.** He is sanctifier, they are sanctified (2:11), and by his self-offering he has opened the way to the heavenly Holy of Holies for them.

10:15-16—Here at the conclusion of his whole central argument the author quotes again from the oracle of Jeremiah (see commentary on 8:8-12). In the oracle we confront something higher than the prophet's intuition or genius, and the ancient word is far more than a religious fossil dug out of the ground of the past. Through the oracle **the Holy Spirit bears witness to us.** And his testimony confirms our author's basic argument of the last paragraphs. The Lord himself promised a new and inward **covenant,** with its stipulations and agreements written not on stone and stored in a wooden ark but inscribed **on their minds** and deposited in **their hearts.**

10:17—The Lord adds a declaration revealing the point, the power, and the wonder of that new covenant: **I will remember their sins and their misdeeds no more.**

10:18—With these words the Lord himself has interpreted the new covenant as entailing full and final **forgiveness,** the entire pardon of all our sins, absolute and unconditional cancellation of the old debt, the total destruction of every barrier to the perfect realization of communion with God.

Where all this has occurred, there simply is no need for any further **offering for sin.** When the real has been attained, no one will turn back to copies and imitations. When worshipers enjoy unimpeded access to the heavenly throne of grace, they no longer depend anxiously on priests in their weakness offering animal sacrifices in tents with hands. They have outgrown all that and have entered a state of spiritual maturity (6:1).

■ Concluding Exhortation: Let Us Draw Near to the Throne of God! (10:19-31)

Draw Near, Hold Fast, Consider (10:19-25)

In Greek verses 19-25 are a single tightly constructed sentence. It is the opening statement in a great series of appeals grounded in the word "hard to explain" (5:11), the "solid food" or "word of righteousness" (5:12) expounded in 7:1—10:18. That teaching for the mature, centering on Jesus as great and final high priest, is quickly summarized in 10:19-21. Then the author derives three exhortations from that teaching: **Let us draw near** (10:22), **let us hold fast the confession** (10:23), **let us consider** (10:24). The first appeal has to do with faith, the second with hope, and the third with love.

10:19—For the first time since Chapter 3 (3:1, 12) the author addresses his readers directly and calls them **brethren.** He expresses his solidarity with them and bridges the distance between himself and them as he opens his final and climactic appeal.

First he restates the blessing he has extracted from his preceding explication of Jesus' high priesthood: **We have confi-**

dence to enter the sanctuary. He has vividly portrayed Jesus' own entrance into the sanctuary, but here focuses on the consequences of Jesus' action for the members of the community. God has presented us with an unspeakable gift by opening wide the path to his own presence, here called the heavenly sanctuary, his dwelling place. It is sheer grace that he summons mere mortals, stained as we are, to his presence. His action and invitation are designed to dispel all hesitation, false modesty, honest shame, or faintheartedness, and to instill confidence or boldness in those with absolutely no claim whatsoever upon God.

The sole ground of confidence is the blood of Jesus. Christ entered the celestial sanctuary with his own blood to deal once and for all with the sins of humanity, annulling sin, destroying its power, purifying the stained, qualifying the disqualified, and simply bestowing upon them the gift of confidence (9:24-26; 10:10-12).

10:20—By his sacrifice Jesus opened for us a new and living way into the sanctuary, so there is after all something genuinely new under the sun (Eccles. 1:9). The Greek word behind opened is translated "ratified" in 9:18. It means to found, to dedicate or to inaugurate with solemn rites and ceremonies.[61] The festival now called Hanukkah bears the Greek name of "Dedication" (John 10:22). The Temple had been captured and desecrated by Antiochus Epiphanes in 165 B.C. and rendered unfit for the worship of the Lord. When the Maccabees regained control, they solemnly purified the temple. They redirected it and inaugurated a new period in its use. With his blood Jesus has dedicated and opened the heavenly sanctuary for our use. Though he died on earth, he lives above.

Since the living one is the means of access to God, the way is living (John 14:6). He is not like the countless dead victims of animal sacrifice at earthly Jerusalem. The way into the sanctuary is through the curtain, that is, through his flesh.

His blood is a bath purifying his people and qualifying them to stand like priests in the presence of the Most High (v. 19;

John 13:10). And his flesh, pierced and violated to release the flow of his life's blood (John 19:34), is like the **curtain** veiling the inner sanctum of the Temple. The Holy of Holies was sometimes even called "the house of the veil" (Sirach 50:5). That veil or curtain was penetrated once each year by the solitary high priest, approaching the mercy seat on behalf of all the people. The curtain of Jesus' flesh has been penetrated and torn once and for all to provide perfect access to God's presence for ever.

Some translations (the NEB, for example) connect **flesh** not with **curtain** (as do RSV and TEV) but with **the new and living way.** They understand the passage to be saying that his **flesh,** his earthly life provided by his incarnation, constitutes **the new and living way** through all barriers and veils to God. In any case, the totality of the self-offering of Jesus, the gift of his flesh and blood, is the new and crucial factor in the granting of access to people once blocked from God's presence by their sin.

10:21—The author has previously been emphatic that Christ was faithful not only "in" but "over" God's house (3:6), and so now he writes that **we have** as gift and secure possession **a great priest over the house of God.** Because of the nature of the sacrifice Jesus offered, because it was effective once and for all, because he sits and needs no longer to stand and repeat his work daily, because the sanctuary he serves is heavenly, and because he so far surpasses earthly priests in the dignity of his person and in the effectiveness of his work, it seems very nearly inappropriate to call him priest. But the author does continue to apply that title to Jesus, however much it may limp. Our best metaphors may be no better than broad hints, but they do manage to reveal at least occasional flashes of the truth.

10:22—Practical consequences should flow from these great assertions of spiritual fact about the blood and flesh of Jesus and his high priestly status. **Let us draw near** to the heavenly tent and throne of God (4:16).

The Greek word behind **draw near** is glimpsed in the English word *proselyte:* one who approaches or draws near and enters another faith family. The same word described the ritual approach of qualified priests to the most sacred precincts of the Temple and to God himself (cf. 12:18, 22), and that is the more likely background here.[62]

The approach must be **with a true heart,** wholeheartedly, with undivided loyalty, **in full assurance** and unwavering conviction (cf. 6:11) **of faith.** Fidelity that is undiluted and unalloyed is alone appropriate to the overwhelming reality of God. That fealty or faith becomes the main theme of the magnificent recitation in Chapter 11.

We are permitted bold approach like priests fresh from their purifying baths because **our hearts,** the depths of our inner being, have been **sprinkled clean from an evil conscience** (9:14; 10:2; 12:24), and **our bodies** have been **washed with pure water.** These are not two washings but one. The whole person, the entire being, in deepest inwardness and in all externalities, has already been washed and purified and rendered fit for access to God by the work of Christ (cf. John 13:6-10). Neither whole oceans nor entire rivers of water, nor any ceremony or hallowed ritual can remove the deep stain of sin. But washings and lustrations served from earliest times to express the sinner's plea for cleanness and to communicate the purifying power of the grace of God.

Priests descended into ritual pools before donning fresh vestments and daring to enter the sanctuary (Lev. 16:4). The ashes of the red heifer were stirred into "the water of impurity, for the removal of sin" (see commentary on 9:13). A great bronze sea stood at the Temple in Jerusalem, an intricate system of water channels and cisterns was constructed at Qumran, and pools for ritual bathing were installed in synagogues. All these bear eloquent witness to human need and to the divine promise of cleansing. It was natural and easy for the first Christians to meditate upon the effects of Jesus' death in terms of washing and purification, and it is no surprise that initiation into the community was accomplished with ablutions (6:2). Because of Jesus—because of the work he accomplished at the cross—the Christians felt clean and then committed themselves to a life of purity.

10:23—A second conclusion is urged on the basis of Jesus' priestly work and status: **Let us hold fast** and not relinquish either willfully or by default **the confession of our hope** first solemnly uttered at our Baptism (cf. 3:1, 6). And our **hope** is nothing less than sharing in Christ (3:14), entering the rest (4:1), and standing before the throne of grace in the heavenly sanctuary (4:16).

Holding our confession **without wavering,** without any eclipse of fervor or confidence, parallels approaching the sanctuary "with a true heart in full assurance of faith" (10:20). If any wavering, weakening, or waffling occurs, it cannot be traced to God, since he **who promised is faithful** and unfailing.

10:24—The first *Let us* (v. 22) dealt with faith and the second (v. 23) with hope. The third urges love: **Let us consider** (cf. 3:1) **how to stir up one another,** how to jab or provoke one another, **to love and good works.** Of course love cannot be provoked (1 Cor. 13:5) in the sense that people cannot be browbeaten into loving, but it can certainly be stimulated.[63]

10:25—To some extent the following words explain how those who share in Christ can stimulate one another, and we get here a glimpse into the author's thinking about the nature of the Christian community. God never forsakes his people (13:5), and they must not forsake one another.

Hard evidence that the Christians were relinquishing the Christian fellowship for that of mystery cults or the worship of angels is lacking but for whatever reason some had fallen into the easy **habit** of **neglecting to meet together.** We do not know the reason for that habit. It may have arisen out of sheer weariness and slackness, or out of an individual sense of superiority over the mass of one's fellow believers, or because of the political danger or social liability entailed in identifying oneself with the Christian movement (10:32f.). The original fires of eagerness and expectation of the climax of cosmic history may have been banked in the second or third generation (2:3; 13:7), and toward the end of the first century and the beginning of the second Christians were attracting unfriendly attention and experiencing the beginnings of persecution under Emperors Domitian and Trajan.

The author began by calling his readers "brethren" (10:19) and continued by reminding them of what had been gained for them by the unflinching endurance of Jesus all the way to the cross.

Now he points them forward and speaks of life lived in view of the kind of future pressing in upon them. Total newness is on the way, and it is impossible or at least illogical to live life as usual or to be too impressed by the powers of the present, no matter how alluring or how threatening, no matter how seductive or how destructive. The readers should **encourage one another,** and do it **all the more as you see the Day drawing near.**

A Fearful Prospect (10:26-31)

Talk of "the Day" (v. 25), the great and final Day when the coming one will reveal himself (10:37), save those who eagerly await him (9:28), and dispense judgment to the others (9:27), leads to a paragraph of sternest warning. The author regularly adds severe warning to his appeals in his admonitory outpourings (cf. 6:6-8).

The alternatives are clear. The blood of Jesus (10:19, 29) can be used in one of two diametrically opposed fashions. Either the community draws near to God on the basis of Jesus' sacrifice, or, spurning the offer, it turns its back on God, thereby signaling that it prefers to remain outside the realm of his grace.

As Hebrews describes the origin or foundation of the Christian community, it frequently combines the image of the new and singular word uttered by God in One who is his Son with

131

that of the purifying power of the Son's self-sacrifice (1:1-3; 2:3). Hebrews has been speaking in cultic terms in 10:19-25 and now speaks of becoming a Christian as **receiving the knowledge of the truth** (cf. 5:11–6:5; cf. John 8:32; 1 John 2:21; 2 John 1; cf. the Pastorals).

Once again in this fresh context the author deals with what happens **if we sin deliberately** (cf. 3:12; 5:2; 6:6). Such sin is unpardonable, for **there no longer remains a sacrifice** for it.

10:27—Deliberate sin and willful disobedience bring in their train neither freedom nor peace but only **a fearful prospect of judgment and a fury of fire** which will consume all those **adversaries** whose power makes Christians question their confession and waver in their resolution.

10:28—The historic principle is well known: under **the law of Moses** certain offenses, deliberate or presumptuous sins (Deuteronomy 1), corroborated by **the testimony of two or three witnesses,** resulted in the execution of the death penalty.

Obviously the author is here dealing with something more pernicious than occasional lapses into sin, more dangerous than sinning accidentally in ignorance or under stress. Those are expected, since he describes Jesus as the high priest who deals gently with our infirmities (2:17-18; 4:15-16; 5:2).

On the basis of these words, rigorists like Tertullian denied the availability of forgiveness for any postbaptismal sin, while more practical or pragmatic-minded people built on these words a penitential system. Both took seriously the holiness of God and the seriousness of sin and strove for purity in the church.

The author of Hebrews is neither a rigorist nor a bureaucrat. What he urges in his appeals and threats is that Christians nourish the bond they enjoy with their great high priest and permit nothing on earth to sever them from him, for apostasy is quite simply fatal.

10:29—In another of his characteristic comparisons the author describes **how much worse punishment** will be the lot of sinners under the new covenant than under the old (cf. 2:2).

Three strong parallel phrases spell out a definition of deliberate sin (cf. 3:12; 6:4-8):

1. To **spurn the Son of God.** That means contemptuously to trample him underfoot (6:6; Zech. 12:3; Matt. 7:6).
2. To **profane the blood of the covenant by which he was sanctified.** That means to defile that absolutely unique and extraordinary sacrifice of Jesus by which alone the Christian is purified and hence qualified to stand before God (9:14-22), to treat it as common and cheap and ordinary, and hence to reject utterly the blessings flowing from it.
3. To **outrage the Spirit of grace.** That means to insult the Spirit (Mark 3:29) and despise God's grace, as though we were fit to stand before God on our own, without grace to qualify us.

10:30—God is neither blind to our disobedience nor indifferent to our sin. Quotation of two lines from the Song of Moses in Deuteronomy 32 underscores the intensity of the author's concern: **Vengeance is mine, I will repay** (cf. Rom. 12:19). **The Lord will judge his people.** In their original context these two lines portray God as Israel's champion, vindicating them against their enemies. But here they function to warn God's people that he punishes rebels.

Vengeance is a harsh word borrowed from broken human relations to describe an aspect of the reality of broken relations between God and his creatures. The God who has spoken the word of salvation in one who is a Son is the same God who **will judge his people** when they turn a deaf ear to his plea or refuse to enter his presence (Deut. 32:36). Infidelity has dire consequences.

10:31—It is indeed **a fearful** (v. 27) **thing to fall into the hands of the living God.** This stern reminder of God's awesome holiness is addressed to the Christian community and is designed to waken them from their careless slumbers and to stiffen their backbones. The harshness of the word may be tempered by the memory that David, when he sinned by tak-

ing a census of the people, chose as his punishment to "fall
into the hand of the Lord, for his mercy is great." But he said,
"Let me not fall into the hand of man" (2 Sam. 24:14).

Strive to Reach the Heavenly Goal! (10:32—13:25)

■ Opening Exhortation and Statement of Theme: You Need Endurance to Do God's Will and Receive What Is Promised (10:32-39)

The author opens the paragraph with an appeal to his
readers to **recall the former days,** to examine the record of
their behavior in the days following their entrance into the
community out of the world of ignorance and darkness, the
days immediately after they were enlightened and first tasted
the heavenly gift and became partakers of the Spirit (6:4). In
those early days the young community **endured a hard struggle with sufferings.** Behind the word **struggle** is the Greek
word transliterated as *athletics.*[64] They had been plunged almost immediately into a hard contest and they had endured
(see commentary on 10:36). Here is one of the few windows
provided by Hebrews into the history of the fellowship.

10:33—What was the nature of the contest or struggle? Like
so many early Christian communities, they were themselves
from time to time **publicly exposed to abuse and affliction.**
These words and images are related to Paul's figurative expression of himself and his fellow apostles as "men condemned to
death in the arena, a spectacle for the whole universe" (1 Cor.
4:9, NEB).[65] And sometimes the readers had become **partners
with those so treated.** These ideas of suffering personal loss
and of aiding the sufferers are taken up in the next verse in
reverse order.

10:34—They did not hide the fact of their faith but openly
had compassion on the prisoners, visiting and supporting those
under arrest in spite of the obvious and real dangers of doing

so. Early Christians displayed a remarkable concern for the imprisoned (13:3). Once before in dangerous circumstances the recipients of Hebrews had habitually expressed solidarity which they were presently in danger of carelessly relinquishing (10:24).

And they also had not merely resigned but **joyfully accepted the plundering** of their **property** by mobs or official confiscation. Material loss did not upset them, **since** (they) **knew that** (they themselves) **had a better possession and an abiding one.** Here **better** and **abiding,** two of the author's favorite words for describing the heavenly realities made available now through Jesus, are linked as synonyms so that they define one another. They are **better** than the old precisely because they are **abiding** and immutable, not transient, fading, and merely earthly. The author places a fresh interpretation on the familiar distinction between the old and the new, the ancient and the current. He is thinking more spatially than chronologically.

10:35—The author urgently appeals to his readers, that they not throw away their former confidence, their boldness, that wonderful courage in which they freely and gladly suffered in the past (v. 34). They should retain that boldness in the face of present adversity (3:6; Acts 4:13) and receive their reward (cf. 11:26; Luke 6:23).

10:36—They endured the tough contest of the past (v. 32) and now again they need to summon up reserves of **endurance.** Without that **endurance,** patience, or fortitude [66] they will not find strength to **do the will of God** in the present or finally **receive what is promised** in the future. Jesus persevered in doing God's will (10:7, 9), enduring suffering, and has been exalted. He is forerunner and coming one.

10:37-38—In order to highlight the new topic and underscore the announcement of it, the author quotes the prophet Habakkuk who urged Israel to live through hard times in **faith** (Hab. 2:3-4). **Faith** here and everywhere in Hebrews is not exactly the same as in Paul. For Paul (Rom. 1:17; Gal. 3:11) the primary meaning of **faith** is grasping and holding

135

fast the promise of what God has already achieved for mankind in the death and resurrection of Jesus. For Hebrews **faith** is fundamentally the endurance and fidelity of holding on as we wait for the final appearing of the coming one. **Faith** in Hebrews is more like what Paul calls hope. It strains forward and upward toward unseen and unchanging realities.[67]

Since verse 35 the author has been turning from his recollection of the past to a consideration of his readers' present spiritual orientation. He looks for confidence, endurance, faith as patient waiting, or even tenacity—the topic of Chapter 11.

10:39—The chapter concludes on a positive and triumphant note. The opposite of faith is shrinking back. **We are not of those,** exults the author, **who shrink back and are destroyed, but of those who have faith and keep their souls.** "By your endurance," Jesus said, "you will gain your lives" (Luke 21:19).

People characterized by a timid trimming of their sails and by holding back are moving towards loss of their lives, but those marked by courageous faith will gain their lives. Chapter 11 is devoted precisely to faith and to the gaining of life.

■ Historical Review: Heroes of Faith and Endurance (11:1-40)

Commentators like to point out that 10:39 continues smoothly in 12:1, and that a reader who simply skipped Chapter 11 would not sense any bumps in the road. While that is true, we should sing a doxology that the author chose to include Chapter 11, because without this material we would be languishing in a state of considerable impoverishment.

It was common practice among ancient philosophers and teachers of all kinds to bolster an argument, justify a stance, or plead for a course of action in the present by calling to the witness stand a series of the heroes of the past. The Wisdom of Solomon (10:1—12:27), without naming names, obviously refers to Adam, Cain and Abel, Noah, Abraham, Lot, Jacob,

Joseph, and Moses in a hymn to wisdom. That hymn is encouragement to live in the present by that same wisdom which shaped Israel's history from the start.

Sirach 44:1–50:21 begins with the celebrated line, "Let us now praise famous men," and lauds ancient worthies beginning with Enoch and Noah, continuing through Zerubbabel, Joshua, and Nehemiah, and climaxing in the priestly rule of Simon the son of Onias (ca. 219-196 B.C.). According to Sirach, wisdom has been the creative principle of life throughout the universe from the first and has become embodied in Torah. True wisdom is fearing the Lord by cherishing Torah and discovering in it God's own power for life and blessing.

The farewell of Mattathias, father of Judas Maccabeus, which is found in 1 Maccabees 2:49-68, rehearses the deeds of the fathers from Abraham to Daniel and urges the readers to kindle the flame of zeal for the Law.

In the Mishhah, a late second-century Jewish document, the tract called "The Sayings of the Fathers" (Pirke Aboth) contains a bouquet of the decisions of the rabbis, arranged not simply to display the truth but to encourage readers to love Torah as the sages of the past did.

1 Clement throughout its 65 chapters begs the Corinthians to attend to the negative and positive examples of Enoch and Noah (9), Abraham and Isaac and Jacob (10 and 31), and Lot (11) and Rahab (12) among others, and to learn from them the destructiveness of envy and discord and the greatness of faith, meekness, and hospitality.

Comparison with those other lists reveals that Hebrews 11 is a history of faith in the unseen, of patience founded on that faith, and of God's approval of faith and patience.

The original biblical accounts alluded to by the author in this chapter rarely mention faith. Elsewhere our author usually argues on the basis of the actual words in the ancient text, but here he offers his own singular reading of the grand sweep of the biblical story. He has meditated on that story and introduced the theme of faith.

The chapter is neatly structured. Between the opening (1-2) and closing (39-40) verses stand 18 examples from the past, beginning with the phrase **by faith.**[68] Four statements cover the period from creation to Noah (vv. 3-7). The next set of seven (vv. 8-22) features Abraham, with an intervening commentary in verses 13-16. In a second set of seven (vv. 23-31) Moses dominates the stage. The author quickly scans the history from the judges to the Maccabees (vv. 32-38) and then brings his recitation to a close (vv. 39-40).

1-2	Statement of theme
3-7	From Creation to Noah
8-22	The Days of Abraham
13-16	A Side Comment on the Story
23-31	The Days of Moses
32-38	A Survey of Additional Examples
39-40	A Concluding Word

Conviction of Things Not Seen (11:1-2)

11:1—The author has just spoken about the mortal danger of shrinking back and has extolled faith as the way to life. He now sings the praises of faith.

Far from shrinking back, **faith** means having confidence, **assurance,** and **conviction** regarding unseen realities. Those realities are described as **things hoped for** (as though they lay still in a chronological future) and as **things not seen** (because they belong to the eternal and unchanging world above).

The second of those pictures seems dominant in the author's mind.

Again, the author does not describe faith in terms of Jesus and his saving work accomplished at the cross and empty tomb as Paul does, but in terms of an eternal and heavenly dimension different from the world of flux open to our senses. The ability to see with our physical eyes produces conviction about visible things; through faith people *see* God, besides gaining conviction about the higher, invisible world. By faith they lay hold upon invisible realities.[69]

11:2—This faith is nothing new. It is no religious novelty, **for by it the men of old,** our own religious ancestors elsewhere called "the fathers" (1:1), themselves **received divine approval** and were given a good report by God. Behind this latter phrase is the word for *witness,* which later became the technical term for a *martyr.*[70] It is an important concept in Hebrews precisely in this context (10:15; 11:2, 4, 5, 39; cf. 7:8, 17). The believers of ancient times become divinely approved witnesses to us (10:28; 12:1). By their lives they testify to the power of faith to shape lives worthy to be emulated.

Abel, Enoch, Noah (11:3-7)

11:3—The historical list of the fathers of faith is prefaced by a mention of creation. The author is more sharply dualistic than the Wisdom of Solomon, which says that the world was made out of formless matter (Wisd. of Sol. 11:17), as a potter shapes his clay (Gen. 2:7; Isa. 64:8; Job 33:6). The world simply did not exist at all until it was summoned forth and **created by the word of God. What is seen** is secondary and transient. It **was made out of things which do not appear** (Rom. 4:17; 2 Macc. 7:28).[71]

This verse sets the tone for the entire list. The appeal is to lift eyes of faith to the sure and unshakeable realities, to the Creator himself, and not to be blinded or dazzled by the transient power of the visible.

11:4—The list of ancestors begins with Abel, the first person in Scripture said to have sacrificed to God, and his sacrifice was **more acceptable** or more pleasing than that of his brother Cain. It must have been, because he **received** divine **approval as righteous** (10:38; cf. Matt. 23:35; 1 John 3:12), and God was quite obviously **bearing witness** to that fact by **accepting his gifts.**

Abel, the first worshiper or first bringer of sacrifice, was the first man to be murdered. **He died** a violent death at his brother's hands, **but through his faith he is still speaking.** He is the one judged right, not only by God, but by every generation in Israel and the church. He and not Cain is lofted before our eyes as example. It is not only that his blood speaks to God (Gen. 4:10; Heb. 12:24; Matt. 23:35) but Abel speaks to us generation after generation of the rightness and the power of faith. That **he died** is not the last word, nor can it ever be on one who is righteous. The righteous are marked not for destruction but for life (10:39).[72]

11:5-6—**Enoch** represents a contrast to Abel, since Enoch, when he was 365 years old (Gen. 5:24), **was taken up so that he should not see death.** Some ancient traditions praise Enoch as seer (1 Enoch; Jude 14–18) and others as sage (Jubilees 4:17), but for Hebrews the vital thing is that Enoch **was attested as having pleased God** by his righteous life (10:38), and that implies faith in God, because **without faith it is impossible to please him.**

Whoever would draw near to God and step into his presence (4:16; 7:25; 10:22) **must believe that he exists and that he rewards those who seek him.** The first part, believing that he exists, is an elementary teaching of the faith (6:1). The accent falls on the second part: believing that God rewards, that God is just, that the quest for God is never ignored, that the voice crying to God never falls on deaf ears, that God has power over the future and that all our futures belong to God. Again in this definition or description of faith there is nothing specifically Christological. God and the character of God are the object of faith.

11:7—That Noah was **warned by God** means that he was the recipient of divine instruction (8:5; 12:25) through oracular or prophetic utterance.[73] That revelation laid open to the eye of his faith **events as yet unseen.** Again faith is not presented as clinging to what Christ has won at the cross, but as seeing the invisible. It is detachment from the world and utter reliance upon God and upon realities not visible to physical eyes. It is not said that Noah was singled out for his wisdom or outstanding morality while the rest of humanity wallowed in ignorance or immorality. Faith is praised, and having eyes fastened on the material world is condemned.

Noah foresaw the flood to come and he perceived God's providence and **took heed. Warned** and **took heed** stand neatly parallel to one another in the original. They emphasize that divine revelation came to Noah and he grasped it in piety and reverence. Together those two terms describe his faith, and on the basis of that faith he took an action which seemed the height of foolishness to the world.

He **constructed an ark for the saving of his household.** That expression of faith on his part constituted a high standard, and, measured by it, **the world** stands shamed and indeed **condemned** or proved wrong (cf. John 16:8).

World here, as in the Johannine writings, means sinful humanity, the world mired in a sink of skepticism and unbelief.

Because he had faith and acted on it, Noah became qualified to enter into possession of **the righteousness which comes by faith.** The faithful person is God's righteous one (10:38).

Abraham Obeyed (11:8-22)

11:8—Abraham, the great father of all the faithful, dominates verses 8-22 which speak of him, his wife Sarah, his son Isaac, grandson Jacob, and great-grandson Joseph. The phrase **by faith** is used seven times in these verses.

The opening verse in the series describes Abraham in a manner paralleling what was just said of Noah. As Noah received the forewarning of divine revelation, Abraham **was called** by the voice of God addressing him (Gen. 12:1; cf. Acts 7:2). As Noah piously built an ark, Abraham **obeyed** and went out from Mesopotamia. As Noah placed his trust in things unseen, so Abraham, in the absence of any physical evidence or hard proof, **went out, not knowing where he was to go.** As Noah became an heir of righteousness as the fruit of his faith, so Abraham, because he was faithful to the call, became heir to a new place. Here again faith is dependence upon

141

realities not available to the senses and not subject to ordinary calculation, and faith leads to action lauded by God's people.

11:9—Abraham entered the land but never did possess so much as one square foot of it, except for the field he purchased from Ephron the Hittite near Hebron to serve as a family burial plot. He only **sojourned in the land** and through all his days it remained for him a land **of promise,** a strange and **foreign land,** one he never had and held as his own. He was destined to wander the length and breadth of it, a stranger in his own land, not able to settle down but always **living in tents,** mere portable and temporary quarters. His son and grandson, the patriarchs **Isaac and Jacob,** like Abraham, were not possessors but **heirs with him of the same** unfulfilled **promise.**

So the realization of the promise was delayed, but Abraham displayed no impatience. He sojourned in the land **by faith.** His grasp of the promise of things unseen sustained him.

11:10—The author indeed implies that Abraham lifted his eyes from any earthly fulfillment of the promise **to the city which has foundations.** Any life, any possession, any construction in the world lacks stable and enduring foundations and is transitory, subject to being shaken to pieces and passing away. The only abiding city (12:22; 13:14) is the one **whose builder and maker is God.**

The author dwells on Abraham's sojourning in tents, portable habitats of skins stretched over poles, obviously lacking foundations and either the look or the substance of permanence. That tent-dwelling of Abraham stands in stark contrast to the settled style of Canaanite city dwellers, but it suited Abraham perfectly. His tent-dwelling aptly expressed his contentment to be a pilgrim and his hope for a better city.

The true rest is not the earthly Canaan to which Joshua led the people (4:8), nor is the **city** of promise any earthly settlement within that land. The true rest and the abiding city belong not to the earthly and temporal order of things but are above, prepared and kept by God.

Abraham received partial fulfillment of his hopes, especially in the gift of a son (6:13-15), but he kept his eyes fixed steadfastly above. **He looked forward;** he lived in expectation.

11:11-12—Sarah herself, or "even Sarah," old as she was, long past her childbearing years, **received power** from God **to conceive.** This wonder occurred **by faith,** and her faith is defined in the phrase: **She considered him faithful who had promised.**

The author seems to ignore the laughter of Sarah and the skepticism of Abraham reported in Gen. 17:17 and describes faith as counting on God to keep his word even in the most impossible of circumstances.

Certain difficulties attend taking the verse as it stands in the RSV. The Greek phrase translated in the RSV as **received power to conceive** really means "received power to deposit seed" and refers not to the woman's act of conceiving but to the man's act of impregnating.[74] Furthermore, verses 10 and 12 clearly speak of Abraham, and as translated by RSV verse 11 constitutes an interruption in the flow of thought.

It is easily possible to construe the underlying Greek in such a way as to yield the following translation:

> By faith he (Abraham) received power to beget a child together with Sarah, even when he was past the age, since he considered him faithful who had promised.[75]

Whichever translation one chooses, the point the author makes is that faith means counting on God to keep his word even in the most impossible of circumstances and in the face of the most stunning counter-indications.

Abraham was not just **past the age** (v. 11). He was **as good as dead** and Sarah's womb was "dead" (Rom. 4:19). Nevertheless, from this **one man,** by the power of God, **were born descendants,** and here the author quotes the words of the promise of God in Genesis, **as many as the stars of heaven and as the innumerable grains of sand by the seashore** (Gen 15:5; 22:17; 32:12).

These All Died in Faith (11:13-16)

These next four verses are a commentary on the preceding five, and they prepare for the next six which pick up the story of Abraham and Sarah, of Isaac and Jacob, and continue it down to that of Joseph.

11:13—**These all** had lived in faith, and they all persevered in faith until they **died in faith,** not dismayed or dissuaded by **not having received what was promised.** Entrance into the promised land, living there in tents, and being gifted with offspring were not the fulfillment of the promise but only encouraging signs of God's enduring faithfulness (see 6:15). They never did actually grasp and hold the promised fulfillment. Indeed, it is not a quantity or thing able to be grasped and held. It belongs to another order of reality. They all died, **having seen it** with eyes of faith and having hailed or **greeted it from afar** (11:39).

Afar designates Canaan, which turns out to be not the promise, but only the far country where they were content to dwell for a time. The patriarchs gladly **acknowledged** their status as passing guests and sojourners (Ps. 39:12), **strangers and exiles** (Gen. 23:4). They paid no heed to the stigma attached to the status of resident aliens and happily spoke of their life **on the earth** as a pilgrimage (Gen. 47:9).[76]

11:14—By means of that language they **make it clear that they are seeking a homeland** even though they lived in the land to which the Lord had led them.

11:15—If they were restless in Canaan, it was not because they had an ache to return to Mesopotamia, **that land from which they had gone out.** They gave no thought to a move in that easy, backward, and nostalgic direction. To be sure, Jacob traveled back to Mesopotamia, but as a fugitive from his brother Esau (Heb. 12:16-17), seeking asylum, or at his mother's behest, seeking a wife among kindred people. In either case he had no intention of settling there.

11:16—The fact of the matter is, both their words and deeds reveal that they reach out in hope and aspiration, longing neither for Canaan nor for Mesopotamia but for **a better country, that is, a heavenly one.** Here is the important and characteristic definition: **Better** means **heavenly.**

Abraham and the patriarchs, in life and death, exhibited a faith corresponding to the faithfulness of God. **Therefore God is not ashamed to be called their God (2:11).** He revealed himself at the burning bush in the declaration, "I am the God of Abraham, the God of Isaac, and the God of Jacob" (Exod. 3:6). The author glimpses the promise of immortality in this ancient self-designation of God (cf. Mark 12:26-27). Far from being ashamed of the patriarchs, God welcomes them into his abiding presence. We know that, because he **has prepared for them a city.** That **city** is nothing different from the "homeland" of verse 14 or the "rest" of Chapters 3 and 4.[77]

Abraham and His Posterity (11:17-22)

These verses climax the narrative of Abraham's faith and offer examples of the faith of Isaac, Jacob, and Joseph.

11:17—In ancient Jewish tradition Abraham endured 10 trials (M. P. Aboth 5:4). The final and supreme test of his faith was the summons to sacrifice Isaac (James 2:21-23). Abraham responded to the call to leave his ancestral home for the promise of a better land (11:8), and in his old age he had miraculously received power to beget a son as partial fulfillment of the promise (11:11). And then **he was tested.** God commanded him to yield up what was most precious in his life. And **by faith** he **offered up Isaac,** carrying fire and knife to Mount Moriah, constructing there an altar out of stones, arranging the wood, binding that only son of his with cords, and stretching him out as a sacrifice on the altar to God (Genesis 22). Abraham stood **ready to offer up his only son** (Gen. 22:2). That final phrase poignantly reflects the special position of this child and the bonds of affection by which he was held. Isaac was the apple of his father's eye. The natural instinct is not merely to preserve but even to indulge the only child.

11:18—Furthermore, would not the death of Isaac spell the death of the promise? He had fathered Ishmael with Hagar, but the revelation had precisely specified that "through Isaac shall your descendants be named" (Gen. 21:12). No Isaac, no descendants, no fulfillment of promise. But Abraham did not draw that quite logical conclusion.

11:19—Abraham operated with a logic of an astonishingly high order. God's demand seemed to contradict and imperil God's promise. God seemed indeed to be at war with God. Nevertheless, Abraham remained convinced that God had the power and the will to accomplish whatever he had promised. Exactly how God would fulfill his promises without Isaac he could not know. God had given to his dead body and to Sarah's dead womb the power to beget a child in old age (11:11), and he was sure that the same God had the power **to raise men even from the dead.**

As a result of this shining faith, Abraham received his son back from the dead, **figuratively speaking.** That is to say, Isaac did not die, but Abraham felt as though he had received his son back from the grave. Or perhaps the phrase should be construed as meaning that Abraham received back Isaac in a manner which prefigured another miraculous return from death, namely Jesus' resurrection.

11:20—A single incident is selected from Isaac's life. He demonstrated his **faith** in the eventual fulfillment of the promise when he **invoked future blessings on Jacob and Esau,** his twin sons (Gen. 27:27-29, 39-40). Again faith is described as confidence in things hoped for, a conviction about things not seen or even seeable with physical eyes (11:1).

11:21—On his deathbed Isaac's son Jacob likewise **blessed each of the sons of Joseph,** Ephraim and Manasseh (Genesis 48). As he did so, he displayed his reverence toward the God of promise, **bowing in worship over the head of his staff** by which he supported himself in his declining years. The powers of physical life faded without his ever grasping the realization of the promise, but his **faith** in the promise and his worship of God remained unswerving and firm.

11:22—The life of Joseph is a drama of reverses and triumphs, but again the author focuses on that moment when the future seemed most bleak and unpromising. **Joseph at the end of his life** did not look backward but, like Isaac, directed his gaze forward in hope. He trusted that God would accomplish **the exodus of the Israelites,** an event that was 400 years in the future. So confident was he that on his deathbed he **gave directions concerning his burial** or more literally "concerning his bones." He made his children swear to carry his mummified remains from Egypt to the promised land (Gen. 50:24-25; Exod. 13:19).

Moses Endured (11:23-31)

11:23—The faith of Moses now begins to dominate the author's story (cf. Acts 7:20-44). Faith was Moses' heritage and his environment from the beginning. Immediately following his birth, **Moses was hid for three months by his parents.** They did not obey **the king's edict.** Pharaoh had solemnly commanded that all male children born to the Israelites must be exposed or drowned at birth in the Nile (Exod. 1:22), but Moses' parents feared God and not the earthly ruler.

Abraham had been commanded to sacrifice his son (11:17) but these parents had a contrary divine directive, and they acted **by faith** to preserve the life of Moses; for **the child was beautiful** to them and to God (Acts 7:20).

11:24—**When he was grown up,** Moses acted **by faith** when he identified himself with the people of promise and rejected the easy life guaranteed a prince in the royal house of Egypt. He **refused to be called the son of Pharaoh's daughter,** who had drawn him from the Nile and adopted him as her own.

11:25—Moses confronted a clear and difficult choice: **share ill-treatment with the people of God** or **enjoy the fleeting pleasures of sin.**

He made the choice of **faith.** What could be more impressively durable than pyramids, the mummies of royalty artfully preserved by priestly craft, and the already ancient empire of the pharaohs? While generations of ancients and moderns were awestruck, Moses counted it all as **fleeting** and transitory, as flowers that bloom for one brief season. The word **fleeting** first appears in the accounts of the endurance of the martyrs in 4 Maccabees (15:2, 8, 23) and came to designate the exact opposite of the word *eternal.*[78]

Moses chose ill-treatment (11:37; 13:3) because he perceived it to be temporary, and he knew the life of his ancestral people to be enduring precisely because they are the people **of God** (11:16). Had he made the contrary choice Moses would have been guilty not only of betraying his people but of the awful sin of apostasy from God, and it is this latter which the author is at pains to combat in his community (10:35; 13:3).

11:26—From his perspective on the far side of the cross and exaltation, the author offers parallels to the phrases employed in the preceding verse. Which is **greater wealth, abuse suffered for the Christ** (13:13) **or the treasures of Egypt** (cf. Phil. 3:7)?

Moses made the choice of faith, and that is the same as saying **he looked to the reward.** He looked away from things visible in all their tantalizing splendor and fixed his gaze solely on the unseen but unshakeable heavenly reward (10:35; 11:6). Blind to the blandishments of earthly wealth and power, Moses acted on the basis of clear spiritual vision.

11:27—Moses' second act of faith has the same structure as the first. **By faith he left Egypt,** and that involved a yes and a no. He said no to the visible king and a magnificent yes to the unseen God. He was **not afraid of the anger** of Pharaoh any more than his parents had been when they hid him after his birth rather than expose him (11:23; but see Exod. 2:14). He feared the only one who deserves to be feared, and so **he endured** and was steadfast in faith and the fear of God, as though he could see him who is invisible as clearly as others can see the pyramids. He went from Egypt to the mountains of Midian, to Sinai, and to an encounter with his God.

11:28—Moses' third act of faith came at the end of 40 years when he returned to Egypt, having been commissioned by God at the burning bush. At the climax of the dread plagues, **by faith he kept the Passover and sprinkled the blood** of the sacrificial lamb on doorposts and lintel so that the angel of death, **the Destroyer of the firstborn, might not touch** the people of God (Exodus 12). The author displays no interest in developing connections between the paschal lambs and the death of Jesus, as he has exploited the correspondences between the ritual of the Day of Atonement and the cross and exaltation.

11:29—As a consequence of that dread night when the firstborn in every Egyptian household died, Pharaoh summoned Moses with Aaron and commanded them to leave the land, together with all the people of Israel (Exod. 12:31). Almost immediately, however, Pharaoh experienced a change of heart and set off in hot pursuit of his Israelite slaves, trapping them between the chariots and the sea (Exod. 14:1-9). In that situation, with perils behind and ahead, Moses lifted up his rod and called for faith, and the Lord got glory over Pharaoh. "At the blast of his nostrils the water piled up, the floods stood in a heap, and the deeps congealed in the heart of the sea" (Exod. 15:8). When surrender and return to slavery looked tempting indeed, **by faith the people** plunged down into the waters and **crossed the Red Sea as if on dry land.** Instead of retreating, the people stepped forward in faith, like Peter stepping out of the boat and walking upon the face of the water (Matt. 14:29). However, **the Egyptians, when they attempted to do the same,** found the wheels of their chariots clogged with mud and were swallowed up by the return of the waters. They went down into the depths like a stone, and all Pharaoh's horses and all Pharaoh's men were drowned for lack of faith.

11:30—A whole generation of Israelites perished in the wilderness for their lack of faith (3:7-19). Then the invasion of the promised land began in earnest, and Israel arrived at the fortified city of Jericho. Victory did not come to Israel because of military prowess or superior tactics. The armed men of Israel merely marched about the city, with priests bearing the ark of the covenant and blowing trumpets of ram's horns. On the seventh day the procession circled the city seven times and on the seventh time, while the priests blew their trumpets, all the people shouted and the walls fell flat, like an avalanche of snow released by the crack of a rifle shot. Not by military might but **by faith the walls of Jericho fell down.**

11:31—When Jericho fell, all the inhabitants, male and female, young and old, animal as well as human, were utterly destroyed and killed, with the single exception of Rahab and her family. **By faith Rahab the harlot did not perish** with all those others who are here described as having been **disobedient.** The clear implication is that Rahab was obedient. She had not only recognized that the future belonged to Israel and to Israel's God, but she had acted on that conviction (James 2:25) and had received the spies in peace as messengers of God. The example of her faith and hospitality won for her an esteemed place in the Jewish and Christian story (Matt. 1:5; Josephus, Antiquities of the Jews 5:7ff; 1 Clement 12:7).

Of Whom the World Was Not Worthy (11:32-38)

The roll call of heroes of faith concludes with a scattered sample of persons and deeds, continuing the story in summary fashion from the days of the judges down through the inauguration of the monarchy and the rise of the great prophets.

Has the author really broken off his more detailed chronicle because **time would fail,** or is that a merely rhetorical flourish? In earlier chapters he broke off his incipient history at roughly the same point. After focusing on angels in the hierarchy of creation (Chap. 1), he discussed God's interest in Abraham and his descendants (Chap. 2), and then continued with interpretations of Moses and Joshua (Chapters 3 and 4). Having gone so far, he declared that "a sabbath rest remains for the people of God" (4:9). He mentioned the entrance into the land as obliquely as possible, hinting at it in the phrase, "If Joshua had given them rest" (4:8). Joshua gave and they received something, but it was not possession of the promise.

The author seems reluctant to continue after the seizure of Jericho. But he drops the names of six ancient worthies: **Gideon, Barak, Samson, Jephthah** from the period of the Judges, **David,** the great founder of Jerusalem's royal dynasty, and **Samuel,** commonly viewed as first among a long and distinguished line of **prophets** (Acts 3:24). It is a curious list, and some of those named were notorious for hesitation, bad judgment, hot temper, or rashness. But the author singles out their **faith** for comment.

In verses 33 and 34 nine short clauses are strung together to describe triumphant activities of faith. Then, in verses 35 to 38, a second series of clauses tersely describes sufferings endured in faith.

11:33-34—Judges and generals, warriors and kings, **through faith conquered kingdoms, enforced justice** or righteousness, and **received promises** of a better kingdom to come. **Through faith** Daniel **stopped the mouths of lions** (especially Dan. 6:22), while Shadrach, Meshach, and Abednego **quenched raging fire** (Dan. 3:28), and these are only some of those who **escaped the edge of the sword** when they were threatened by kings and queens. Elijah made good his escape from Jezebel (1 Kings 19:1-8) and Elisha from her son Jehoram (2 Kings 6:31—7:2).

All these and others—though few in number (Gideon with his 300) or small in stature and tender in years (David before Goliath) or sorely lacking in political clout (Daniel and his fellow exiles)—**through faith won strength out of weakness, became mighty in war, put foreign armies to flight.** These last three phrases are particularly apt as a description of the Maccabees, that small band who struggled successfully against the superior numbers of the Syrian military establishment in the second century B.C.

11:35—Through the prophets Elijah and Elisha the poor widow of Zarephath and the rich woman of Shunem **received their dead** children back again **by resurrection** (1 Kings 17; 2 Kings 4). For others like the Maccabean martyrs (2 Maccabees 6–7; 4 Maccabees 5–17), escape from death could have been purchased by eating a bit of pork (see on 12:1). It seems a cheap price to pay, but they preferred to be **tortured,** even racked and beaten to death with iron bars (2 Maccabees 6). They steadfastly refused **to accept release** offered to them if it involved committing apostasy. They despised easy escape and instead endured, **that they might rise again to a better life,** or literally "enjoy a better resurrection."

It would be **better** than the resurrection enjoyed by the young men of Zarephath and Shunem, in that it would mean not just a temporary stay of the power of death but a final victory over the whole realm of death and dying. It would mean entrance into endless life with God.

11:36-37—The author, in this catalog of horrors, is heaping up the names of every manner of torture and execution he can think of as he concludes his appeal. He may not have had particular historical episodes in mind, although it is possible to attach specific names to some of the punishments.

Before these martyrs actually died they were subject to **mocking and scourging** (2 Maccabees 7; cf. Jeremiah 20; 37), **chains and imprisonment,** and some were **stoned** (2 Chron. 24:20-22; Matt. 23:35). According to ancient tradition Isaiah was **sawn in two** during Manasseh's reign (Ascension of Isaiah 5:1-14). Some like Elijah escaped the edge of the sword (11:34), but others, likewise prophets of the Lord, were felled by Jezebel's fury (1 Kings 19:10). Jeremiah was delivered from Jehoiakim, but the prophet Uriah was dragged back from Egypt and was **killed** at the king's command (Jer. 26:23).

Not all lost their lives. Many lived, but less like humans than like wild beasts, hounded by their enemies. Unpopular prophets dressed **in skins of sheep and goats**[79] and as often as not were **destitute, afflicted, ill-treated.**

Many in the days of Antiochus Epiphanes fell by the sword (Dan. 11:33); others fled to the wilderness (1 Macc. 2:29-38).

They were despised by the world as not fit to live, but in a parenthetical phrase the author lauds them as people **of whom the world was not worthy.**

In the book of Wisdom the righteous are described as those whom God has tested and found worthy of himself (Wis. 3:5). In times when God and the world have collided, the pious have become quite literally people **wandering over deserts and mountains,** driven from their settled lives in homes and shops and reduced to eking out an existence **in dens and caves of the earth,** the lairs of animals (cf. Matt. 8:20).

The beginning of Chapter 12 shows that the sufferings of Christ are in the mind of the author. Nevertheless he does not say what some early Christian writers said. He does not say that "Christ has suffered from the beginning of time in all sufferers, in Abel murdered by his brother, in Noah hated by his son, in Abraham the exile, in Isaac the sacrifice, in Jacob cheated by his uncle, in Joseph sold into slavery, in Moses exposed as an infant and a fugitive as an adult, in prophets stoned and cut to pieces, in apostles wandering on land and adrift at sea." [80]

Well Attested by Their Faith (11:39-40)

11:39-40—**All these** people, patiently enduring the suffering heaped upon them, were **well attested by their faith.** They established an impressive record for themselves as people of faith. Their deeds are not written in heaven's book alone, but in the memories of quite earthly communities, stored up for the encouragement and emboldening of the generations. Nevertheless, as faithful and loyal as they were, they **did not receive what was promised.** Why not? Nothing was lacking in their faith. From beginning to end the record extols their faithfulness. They did not immediately obtain the promise because God had a plan. His design was to delay the fulfillment of the promise, to delay the coming and exaltation of Christ, until the readers might share in it.

God in his providence **had foreseen something better for us** and for them, namely **that apart from us they should not be made perfect.** The faithful of the past were granted a vision of the final perfection. They enjoyed the magnificent prospect of the final reward and foresaw it. But it has been realized in the time of the author in the perfecting of Jesus, in his exaltation to the right hand of the Majesty on high.

The word spoken in these last days is singular, clear, and compelling. For a while trials come and threaten to sweep us away, but the example of the faithful of the past should stiffen our resolve and wakefulness.

Now that Christ has pierced the heavens and entered the sanctuary once and for all, those ancient worthies have been perfected. Therefore their faith should encourage us. We have free and full access to God: better hope, better promises, better covenant, better sacrifices, better possession, better resurrection (7:19, 22; 8:6; 9:23; 10:34; 11:35).

■ Exhortation: Let Us Run Our Race! (12:1-17)

Chapter 10 concluded with an appeal for endurance. Now, after the stirring recitation of the names and deeds of heroes of faith and endurance, Chapter 12 resumes the appeal.

Pioneer and Perfecter of Our Faith (12:1-2)

The opening verses of the chapter are packed with some of the chief themes of Hebrews: faith as perseverance or endurance, Jesus as forerunner, pioneer, perfecter, and as one who is sitting at God's right hand.

Verses 1 and 2 constitute a single complex sentence. The first half concentrates on **us** and is a strong appeal for faithful living. The second half focuses on **Jesus** and sums up much of the Christological teaching of Hebrews. With these verses the author has forged an iron link between his ethical exhortation and his doctrinal teaching.

12:1a—The Greek language has many words to introduce inferences or conclusions drawn from preceding arguments and evidence. The very strongest of those terms lies behind the **therefore** at the beginning of this paragraph.[81] The author has just recited the story of great ancient heroes of faith, and he will not let that story go to waste. He hastens to draw a practical lesson from it.

The whole of Chapter 11 lives in his statement that **we are surrounded by so great a cloud of witnesses.** He has listed 16 by name and has spoken broadly of "the Israelites," "the people," "the prophets," "women," "some," and "others."

All these constitute a vast throng, and though apparently dead they still serve a vital purpose: they are a **cloud of witnesses.** It may be that our author pictures them as spectators, sitting in the bleachers watching Christians run their race, keeping their eyes on them. But another interpretation is at least as likely. The author certainly regards those heroes of the past as "well attested by their faith" (11:39), people who bear the stamp of God's approval because of their faithful endurance, people who bear witness to the greatness of faith, people whose stories must surely inspire faith and perseverance. They have borne witness in their own lives to the grandeur of faith, and so their lives cheer the readers on.

The main verb in this long sentence (12:1-2) is the exhortation **Let us run!** Before and after our author, many ancient writers, including the apostle Paul, used an athletic contest as a metaphor for spiritual and ethical struggle (see note on 10:32). However, not only the imagery but even the very phrases here are astonishingly close to those of 4 Maccabees, a document produced around A.D. 40 in Alexandria or Syrian Antioch, and it is worthwhile summarizing some of the phrases they share for the sake of comparison.

4 Maccabees tells the story of Jewish martyrs in the grim days of Antiochus Epiphanes. Antiochus of Syria persecuted observant Jews and, in the effort to compel them to renounce the law of Moses and eat the flesh of swine, he produced a bumper crop of martyrs.

Those Jewish martyrs "despised" the tortures Antiochus inflicted upon them and bore up under the torments like athletes taking the punishment which training entails. All humankind and indeed the entire universe were "spectators" of their struggle. They "kept their eyes steadfastly raised to heaven" and "looked away (from the sweet earth and from bodily torments) to God." [82] They endured insults and terrible pain, and ultimately gained victory in their contest with Antiochus.

By their "endurance" they gained "the victor's crown" of life and stand now beside the throne of God. They hastened to death by torture as if running the path to immortality.

In strikingly similar language the readers of Hebrews are urged like athletes to **lay aside every weight.** Any encumbrance whatsoever to the running of the race must be rudely cast aside. Clothing can weigh runners down, hold them back, cramp their style, and impede the free movements of their limbs, so athletes in the ancient Greek world customarily trained and competed in the nude.

Without entering into any details, the author makes it clear that in talking about **weight** and excess baggage, he speaks of **sin which clings so closely.** Sin wraps itself around our lives more closely than clothing, so it binds, constricts, and inhibits running a good race. Some ancient manuscripts use here a similar word meaning "terribly distracting." [83] In either case Hebrews has from the beginning spoken of sin as the dread and terrible barrier to the presence of God (1:3; 9:28).

The author summons his readers to **run with perseverance the race that is set before us.** Behind **perseverance** is the same Greek word sometimes translated as "endurance" or "fortitude" (10:36; cf. Luke 21:19). It is the same term used of "the patience of Job" (James 5:11; cf. Rom. 8:25).[84]

The Readers' Situation

Were the original readers suffering persecution? It might seem so because of all the echoes of Maccabean martyrdom and all the talk of cross and shame and painful discipline in these chapters. However, that language, literally describing the experience of ancient worthies and of Jesus, is used figuratively of the readers. They were locked in a struggle all right, but with sin, not with persecutors. While prophets, martyrs, and Jesus himself had shed their blood, the readers had not done so (12:4). They were stricken by a past flurry of persecution and bore up well under most trying circumstances (10:32-34). But now they were in danger of falling from faith, far from the goal, out of sheer lassitude and lack of endurance.

The author is trying to rouse his readers from lethargy in their contest with sin by reminding them of how much more painfully their predecessors suffered and how much more valiantly they strove.

12:2—In the second half of the sentence attention shifts from the readers to Jesus and the path he traveled.

The martyrs of 4 Maccabees "looked to heaven" or "lifted their eyes to God." The author of Hebrews challenges his readers to get busy **looking to Jesus,** literally "looking away from" other objects so as to fasten their attention on Jesus and have eyes for him alone. This picture is new and emphatic, but the author has previously employed other terms for attending to Jesus (2:9; 3:3).

They should attend to Jesus in his capacity as **the pioneer and perfecter of our faith** or fidelity (cf. 3:1-6).

Jesus exhibited exemplary faithfulness in his earthly life (2:13, 17; 3:1-6), raced as pioneer or forerunner along the upward path, and entered as high priest on our behalf into the inner shrine behind the curtain (6:19-20). He has crossed the finish line and achieved the goal. He has breasted the tape and stepped beyond the world of striving and suffering into the unshakeable world of perfection.

Fidelity, loyalty, and patience are fully realized, brought to fullest flower in Jesus, but he does more than perfectly embody the desired faithfulness. In the completeness of his fidelity, Jesus draws us along the same path toward the same victorious goal and so is **perfecter of our faith.**

The greatness of his faith is glimpsed in relation to the magnitude of his suffering. He **endured the cross.** That cruel instrument is named only here in the entirety of Hebrews. Nowhere in ancient literature except in the writings of the

Christian community is the cross ever anything except the most foul and despicable engine of degradation and destruction. Good never flows from it nor is it ever lifted high as a metaphor for sacrifice or service.[85]

Hebrews avoids calling people to "take up" their cross. But the author does summon Christians to run their race behind the one who patiently endured crucifixion.

Did Jesus choose the cross "instead of" choosing some earthly ease, some earthly beguiling **joy that was set before him**? Or did he go to the cross and bear up under its crushing torments "for the sake of" or "in order to gain" the high delight of **joy** in heaven?

Is **the joy that was set before** Jesus the sweetness of life upon God's earth, or is it the crown of victory in the world above? Probably the latter (cf. 2:8-9; John 17:13). The "for" in the phrase **for the joy** is the same as the one in verse 16: "for a single meal." Jesus and Esau had alternatives set before them and their choices were precisely opposite (see commentary on 12:16-18).[86]

Jesus went all the way to the ignominy of the cross, **despising the shame.** It is not that he could easily disregard it, but that he was contemptuous of it and did not permit it to block him from going his faithful way.

The consequence of the unimpaired integrity of his running is that he now **is seated at the right hand of the throne of God.**

Our author exults in Jesus' session at God's right hand and interprets that sitting as the best possible news (1:3; 8:1; 10:12).

He Disciplines Us for Our Good (12:3-11)

12:3—The author calls readers not merely to **consider** but to compare their handling of their situation with **him who endured from sinners such hostility against himself.**

In pointing back to the cross (12:2) by means of the word **such,** and by introducing the word **hostility** or rebelliousness, he underscores the outrageous indignity of the end of the earthly life of the one through whom the worlds were made.

The comparison should not only be sobering but should wake up and embolden readers who have grown **weary or fainthearted.** The same word translated here as **fainthearted** stands behind "lose courage" in verse 5 (cf. Gal. 6:9).[87] The author worries that his readers are at the point of exhaustion, like runners who collapse after crossing the finish line. But the addressees have not yet completed their race! Weariness and weakness beset them a long way from the goal and cast into doubt their ever attaining it.

Hard as they have run, serious as their sufferings undoubtedly were (10:32-33), heroic as their struggles have been—and here the writer moves to the picture of military combat—they **have not yet resisted to the point of shedding** their **blood.** Not yet have the readers struggled so mightily that they have suffered wounds like troops in warfare.[88] Jesus did, and so did many of the heroes named in Chapter 11.

12:5—Now, changing the image once more, our author reminds his readers that they are after all **sons** or children of God, and that has its obvious implications.

Sufferings and hardships are not merely negative experiences to be avoided at all costs. They are **the discipline of the Lord.** Proverbs declares, **The Lord disciplines him whom he loves.** That word throws a new and positive light onto the old face of hardship. "Those whom I love, I reprove and chasten," says the Lord of the church (Rev. 3:19). Earthly parents, overseeing the education and development of their heirs into responsible adulthood, discipline their children. Children demanding instant gratification may rebel against restraints, but responsible parents do not allow their children to grow like wild plants in a patch of weeds.

Likewise it is a matter of **discipline** and for the sake of education and development that the readers **have to endure** hardships patiently, understanding that **God is treating** them **as sons,** as legitimate and beloved offspring.

Especially poignant is the question, **What son is there whom his father does not discipline?** The expected answer is that every child is disciplined. That is emphasized in the phrase about **discipline in which all have participated.** Surely Jesus himself is here in view as one who himself, "although he was a Son, learned obedience through what he suffered" (5:8).

12:8—If no hardships came their way, they might indeed question whether God really cared about them and their growth. It was common enough in the ancient world for a man to father both legitimate and illegitimate children and to prepare the legitimate child of his carefully chosen lawful wife to be his heir by means of a series of tutors and a rigorous program of study and exercises for mind and body. Meanwhile he relegated the illegitimate child to a life of careless ease. Discipline was therefore a sign at once of legitimacy and of selection for inheritance.

12:9-10—We had, writes the author, **earthly fathers to discipline us and we respected them.** In retrospect, at least, children grant the wisdom of hard lessons and see the love in and behind the discipline. It was for our own good. **Much more** should we **be subject to the Father of spirits and live.**

In the Greek original **earthly fathers** is literally "fathers of our flesh," and that phrase stands in parallel with **the Father of (our) spirits.** What is meant is that as we have an earthly, physical father, so have we also one who is heavenly and spiritual, and both of them, if they really care about the direction and shape of our lives, will discipline us.

12:10—Be subject to the heavenly parent **and live,** he says. What is the content of this word **live?** Earthly parents **disciplined us for a short time** during the days of our minority, and they doubtless made mistakes, and sometimes their discipline was willful or capricious. Not so with God's dealings. God **disciplines us for our good,** to our advantage, and the **life** (v. 9) we gain is one in which **we share his holiness.**

12:11—In spite of all his best arguments the author acknowledges that for as long as we live in the midst of this seductive world and in these bodies, vulnerable to a thousand assaults, **all discipline seems painful rather than pleasant.**

But in the end those who are trained in the school of discipline acquire **the peaceful fruit of righteousness.** They progress beyond all resentment and perturbation to victorious contentment, and they live in the world as befits children of God and heirs of heaven.

Lift Your Drooping Hands (12:12-17)

The author had switched from athletic imagery (12:1-2) to metaphors of parenting and education (12:3-11), and now he returns to athletics with words derived from Isaiah and from Proverbs.

The prophet had encouraged exiles in Babylon to **lift your drooping hands and strengthen your weak knees** (Isa. 35:3), to shake themselves out of their depression, to cease their self-pitying, and to prepare to run toward the goal. Especially should the heartier cheer on the discouraged.

12:13—And the stronger should **make straight paths** for the feet of the weak, **that the lame may not be put out of joint** and dislocated **but be healed** (Prov. 4:26). Unless they are full of care, conditions in the community will deteriorate.

12:14—Jesus pronounced his beatitude on the peacemakers (Matt. 5:9) and Paul elevated "peace and grace" to new spiritual and literary prominence in the opening salutations of his letters. When our author urges his readers to **strive for peace with all** people, he is not mouthing platitudes or counseling innocuous behavior but is setting before them the challenge of strenuous action on behalf of the spiritual health and wholeness of the community and of forgiving openness toward outsiders, including even persecutors.

They must aim as well for the **holiness without which no one will see the Lord.** That sounds like Jesus' other beatitude on the pure in heart as the ones destined to see God (Matt. 5:8), and it recalls words in the preceding paragraph about how God disciplines us that we may "share his holiness" (12:10) and enjoy "the peaceful fruit of righteousness" (12:11). The world is alluring in its sweetness and can deal harshly with those who lift their eyes beyond things tangible and transient to God and his unshakeable throne (cf. 12:1-2). The author knows that as well as his readers, but he urges them once more to practice the holiness granted to them by their great purifier (cf. 1:3).

12:15—**See to it** sounds tame, since the author uses a word traditionally associated with the task of philosophers and later reserved for bishops as "overseers" and "guardians." [89] He is calling on members of the community to "look out for" one another and to exercise mutual spiritual supervision so that three dread possibilities may be avoided. The first is falling short of **the grace of God.** He has warned previously of the grave danger of falling away from the living God (3:12) and of failing to enter God's promised rest (4:1). God is seated upon "the throne of grace" (4:16) and is prepared to bestow grace in time of human need. However, receiving God's grace in vain (2 Cor. 6:11) or failing to gain access to the throne of grace remain as terrible possibilities.

Secondly, look after one another, says the author, **that no root of bitterness spring up and cause trouble.** In the original Old Testament context, **root of bitterness** meant the noxious weed of idolatry (Deut. 29:18). Apostasy or turning away from the living God was not impossible (3:12). By that particular weed **the many,** that is, the community in its entirety, could **become defiled.**

And finally they are to watch over one another so **that no one be immoral or irreligious like Esau.** Why like Esau? Why not simply say that any sexual immorality or fornication or adultery, or any impiety, profanity, or godlessness can poison the life of the community? Esau's sin is defined: he **sold his birthright for a single meal.** He exchanged the spiritual for the material, the heavenly for the earthly. Genesis puts it casually but better: he "despised" his spiritual birthright (Gen. 25:34) and traded it cheaply for a quick fix of physical satisfaction.

12:17—This verse is a parenthetical remark regarding Esau, deepening the urgency of the author's appeal. In the end Esau bitterly regretted his fateful decision. He would have given anything to inherit the blessing of the firstborn son, but it was gone forever and could not be recovered, **though he sought it with tears.** His prayer was evidently as earnest as Jesus' own (5:7), but it came too late.

It is folly to count on being able to turn the clock back, and it is spiritual frivolity to live as though present deeds can later be recalled (6:4).

■ Exhortation: You Have Come to Mount Zion. Do Not Refuse Him Who Is Speaking (12:18-29)

You Have Come to Mount Zion and the City of the Living God (12:18-24)

Verse 18 opens with the conjunction **for.** The author now grounds his preceding exhortations about lifting hands and making paths straight and striving for peace and consecration.

The alternatives set before Jesus (12:2) and before Esau (12:16-17) constitute a parable of the situation of the readers. They too must choose either the earthly or the spiritual, the transient or the enduring. Will they choose joy forever or the bread of a single meal? But the choice is now worded in the contrast between two mountains: Sinai and Zion.

Both are terrible in majesty. They do indeed represent two entire orders of existence, the two worlds everywhere in collision in the letter to the Hebrews. Each signifies a message of awesome proportions for humanity. But these mountains do not bespeak Paul's familiar contrast between legalistic demand and gracious promise, between the law and the gospel. Rather they signify the visible and the invisible, earth and heaven, time and eternity. The chronological contrast of old and new, of past and future, which informs Paul's thought, also appears in Hebrews, but it is for all practical purposes absorbed into the spatial scheme of above and below, eternity and time.[90]

12:18-19—These verses recall the picture of 2:2-4 where the author contrasted the awesome "message declared by angels" at Sinai with the even greater message of salvation "declared at first by the Lord and . . . attested to us by those who heard him." Here he paints the portrait of the revelation at Sinai with words derived ultimately from Exodus 19–20 and Deuteronomy 4, focusing on the audible, visible, and tangible character of the event.

When the earlier revelation and elder covenant were delivered to the people of Israel, Mount Sinai, formed aeons ago of granite that most certainly may **be touched,** was wrapped in **a blazing fire, and darkness and gloom and a tempest, and the sound of a trumpet.** The mountain blazed like a gigantic overheated kiln or belching volcano. Gloom as of smoke or storm clouds shrouded its summit, and thunder pealed like the trumpets of judgment day. And the entire awesome display was in the service of a **voice whose words made the hearers entreat that no further messages be spoken to them,** so holy, so glorious, so terrifying was that word.

12:20—The emphasis falls on the material character of the theophany, on its sheer physicality. It belongs to **what has been made** and what is therefore shakable and destined for **removal** (v. 27). Thus the author's description is focused not so much on underscoring the majesty or holiness of the first covenant as on demonstrating with words of Scripture that Sinai was touchable and that it therefore represents a lower level of reality, as holy as that mountain may have been.

Of all the commandments issued at Sinai, the only one here repeated is this: **If even a beast touches the mountain, it shall be stoned.** That mountain belongs with things seen (11:1) or made with hands (9:11, 24). That mountain and the entire first covenant belong to this lower creation (9:11).

12:21—The quoted commandment of course signals the holiness of the mountain and of that moment, so tremendous that even Moses said, **I tremble with fear.** But Sinai is to Zion as shadow to reality.

12:22-24—Christians **have come to Mount Zion and to the city of the living God, the heavenly Jerusalem.** On Mount Zion

stood the city of Jerusalem, focus of the political and religious
life of Israel. Jerusalem was the home of the temple and so
was the goal of pilgrimage for festival throngs assembled to
offer sacrifice and renew their life as God's own people.[91]

Jerusalem early came to signify heavenly realities in the
Christian communities. Paul spoke of "the present (earthly)
Jerusalem" and of "the Jerusalem above" (Gal. 4:25-26) in a
contest where Sinai and earthly Jerusalem are equivalents,
together signifying the old rule of law. For the author of the
Apocalypse, Mount Zion is a heavenly place where the Lamb
stands with the great throng of the blessed, as it sings its song
before the throne and the four living creatures (Rev. 14:1),
and new Jerusalem is a holy city existing from all eternity in
heaven, descending at the end to the new earth as the habitation of the redeemed (Rev. 21:2).

It is not earthly mountains or tangible sanctuaries which
the readers have attained, but to higher and better realities.
The author names them in an impressive list of parallel
phrases: **You have come,** he writes, (1) **to Mount Zion and the
city of the living God, the heavenly Jerusalem,** (2) **to innumerable angels in festal gathering and to the assembly of the
first-born who are enrolled in heaven,** (3) **to a judge who is
God of all and to the spirits of just men made perfect,** and (4)
**to Jesus, the mediator of a new covenant, and to the sprinkled
blood that speaks more graciously than the blood of Abel.**

He pictures (1) a new city, (2) a place of political council
and sacred assembly, (3) ruled by God alone, (4) through Christ
as priest and victim. That may be spelled out at somewhat
greater length:

(1) Mount Zion and the holy city are (2) the heavenly habitation of ten thousand times ten thousand angels (Deut. 33:2;
Dan. 7:10; Rev. 5:11) and of a great uncounted choir of
elect humanity whose names are written in the book of life
(Rev. 21:27). (3) That heavenly city is ruled by no abstract
principle or law but by the living God, personally engaged
with creation as judge of all. God is attended by saints of old

now justified and perfected in surprising fashion, *(4)* for at God's right hand sits Jesus, present not alone as mediator and priest of a fresh covenant (7:22; 9:15), but as victorious victim, who has by his death opened a new path of free access to God.

The end of the series is its climax. The readers are proselytes to Jesus,[92] and he is described as a sacrificial victim whose blood was sprinkled—not merely poured out upon the ground in a senseless act of fratricidal violence—but sprinkled upon a heavenly altar in a heavenly sanctuary.

Do Not Refuse Him Who Is Speaking (12:25-29)

The grand reminder of their spiritual situation is followed hard by an earnest exhortation that they **not refuse him who is speaking** to them in that priest and victim from heaven's high ramparts.

The ancient community did not escape (cf. 2:3) when they disobeyed the message declared by Moses and the angels. That message was **on earth,** an earthly word from an earthly mountain, hardly comparable in grandeur to the word which is **from heaven.** At Sinai, God's **voice then shook the earth** (Exod. 19:18), but a more terrible time is fast approaching when God will, according to the promise, **shake not only the earth but also the heaven** (Hag. 2:6; Isa. 13:13).

In this instance **heaven** is not the unchangeable opposite of transient earth but is instead a segment of the created world (cf. 1:10). God created heaven and earth and the things under the earth, and will **yet once more shake** them. What is promised is the destruction or removal of **what is shaken,** and not merely their transformation. The whole visible world will vanish **in order that what cannot be shaken may remain,** so that finally only the spiritual reality of God's kingship and the heavenly city will abide alone and unrivaled forever. The tangible world, apparently so durable and so trustworthy, will grow old and be discarded like a tattered garment; the works of God's hand will perish, but God remains (1:10-12).

Through Jesus God has brought people to **a kingdom that cannot be shaken,** to a new order, to a fresh spiritual reality. It exists even now as a separate order of reality, unseen, untouched and untouchable, not made by any human hand, not of this creation. It has been received as a gift, and the author summons to a gratitude shaped by a due sense of the majesty of God expressed in the offering of **acceptable worship with reverence and awe.**

12:29—**Our God** is pure mercy, the God of peace (13:20), and at the same time he is **a consuming fire** (cf. 10:27).

■ Final Exhortation: Brotherly Love and Other Advice (13:1-17)

The theological argument and ethical exhortation of Hebrews achieve a stunning crescendo at 12:29. In comparison, Chapter 13 strikes many a reader as a casual miscellany of unrelated moral maxims (1-17), a shotgun exhortation, unfocused bits and pieces of ethical advice fired at random, finally rounded off with personal greetings and a traditional benediction (18-25).

The character of the final chapter, so different from all the preceding, has led to various conjectures: the chapter was originally an independent composition added to commend the work in its entirety as a Pauline letter and to warrant its inclusion in the canon or to give the preceding chapters the Pauline imprimatur. Nevertheless, whatever literary or theological reason exists for labeling Chapter 13 a late addition or an early afterthought, it still inhibits inner coherence and vital connection with the preceding chapters.

Brotherly Love (13:1-6)

13:1—The first brief sentence is simplicity itself: **Let brotherly love continue.** It has neither conjunction nor participles to complicate it or to connect it with the preceding paragraph. It announces a new topic, **brotherly love,** mutual affection within the community, and that topic stands like a title over the opening paragraph of the chapter.

At first glance the paragraph seems to promote five distinct virtues: love, hospitality, compassion, chastity, and contentment. It is possible, however, that the writer structured the paragraph on the basis of four couplets, each of which is followed by a supporting comment. In abbreviated form:

1. Let love continue.
   Show hospitality
   (for thereby some have entertained angels).
2. Remember those in prison
   and those ill-treated
   (since you also are in the body).
3. Let marriage be held in honor.
   Let the marriage bed be undefiled
   (for God will judge).
4. Keep free from love of money.
   Be content
   (for he has said, I will never fail you).

So we may be dealing not with five unrelated virtues but with a carefully structured set of couplets, describing life within the Christian community.[93]

That numerous cities in the ancient and modern worlds bear the name "Brotherly Love" (Philadelphia) is one indication of the cherished standing of this ideal. It appears frequently in New Testament lists of virtues (Rom. 12:10; 1 Thess. 4:9-10; 1 Peter 1:22; 1 John 3:16-17).

In the appeal for such love, the author uses one of his favorite terms. Let it **continue,** he writes, but the verb might better be rendered "abide" or "endure" (cf. 6:19; 10:24, 32-34). It is the identical verb Paul uses of the eternal abiding of faith, hope, and love in 1 Cor. 13:13.

13:2—Among the ancients of the Mediterranean world **to show hospitality to strangers** was a religious and not merely a social obligation (Matt. 25:35; Romans 12-13; 1 Peter 1:4-9).

Greeks recounted the tale of how Zeus appeared in the guise of a weary traveler at the humble dwelling of Philemon and Baucis (alluded to in Acts 14:11), while Jews and Christians remembered how Abraham had **entertained angels unawares** by the oaks of Mamre, receiving the three strangers and refreshing them (Genesis 18).

One of the stated prerequisites of a Christian bishop or elder was that he be hospitable (1 Tim. 3:2; Titus 1:8). Hospitality was especially important in a world where inns and public lodgings were notoriously disreputable, dangerous to life, health, and morality.

13:3—If inns were bad, prisons were immeasurably worse, and Christians knew prisons from the inside. Persecution is hinted at here once again. At some time in the past members of the community had suffered in a hard struggle, enduring public abuse and affliction, the plundering of property and imprisonment (10:32-34). All that had occurred in former days immediately after their conversion, but persecution may have hung over their heads not only as threat and possibility, but also at least in some cases as present experience.

To avoid sharing the fate of those condemned to prison and maltreated, erstwhile friends often faded from sight at the first sound of the rattling of chains. The temptation was to avoid and to forget, and so the appeal is to **remember those who are in prison, as though in prison with them,** feeling their needs as though they were one's own. To **remember** meant providing food and other necessities, paying money to secure their redemption, visiting and praying for the prisoners.

The appeal to remember is broadened to include any and all **those who are ill-treated.** In 11:37 prophets suffering such outrages as mocking, scourging, chaining, imprisonment, and stoning are called **ill-treated.**

Remember them, says the author, **since you also are in the body.** He is not reminding them that they are in the body of Christ. That powerful picture of the church belongs to Paul but is nowhere presented in Hebrews. This work speaks eloquently of our high priest who can sympathize with us, since he shared not only our flesh and blood but also the temptations to which the flesh is heir (2:14-18; 4:14-16). So we also sympathize with prisoners and the oppressed.

13:4—Marriage is to be **held in honor among all,** and **the marriage bed** must be **undefiled.** Married life is mentioned only here in Hebrews. Since this work otherwise maintains an unbroken silence regarding marriage, even though it is full of ethical admonition on other topics, it has been suggested that the people addressed in Chapters 1-12 constituted a monastic community.[94] However, the author nowhere exalts celibacy. Nor, on the other hand, was he involved in protesting against an ascetic avoidance of sexual relations.

If mutual love (v. 1) is in some sense the overriding topic of this paragraph, then verse 4 spells out its meaning for married people. In writing to Macedonian Christians (1 Thess. 4:3-6), Paul directly links love for the fellow Christian and sexual purity. Gentiles in the ancient world did not naturally or traditionally connect religious observance and sexual purity. The church's success in penetrating the Gentile world necessitated confronting issues of sexual behavior, and it did so forthrightly and with candor. The warning that sexual transgression brings divine judgment in its train belongs to traditional Christian teaching (Col. 3:5-6; Eph. 5:6).

13:5—It should occasion no surprise that the paragraph considers first marriage and then money. Ancient ethical discourses, both in the Bible and beyond, regularly mention sexual immorality and love of money in the same breath (see Testament of Jude 18; 1 Cor. 5:10-11). Philo traced the sensuality of Sodom to its material wealth, and such judgments are still not uncommon. Among the qualifications of a bishop are not only that he be hospitable (see v. 2), but that he also be "married only once" and "no lover of money" (1 Tim. 3:2-3). Hebrews urges, **Keep your life free from love of money, and be content with what you have.** Paul called the "love of money" the root of all evil (1 Tim. 6:10), and he noted that godliness has contentment as its companion, just as covetousness is allied to idolatry (1 Tim. 6:6; Col. 3:5).

It is beyond possibility to serve both God and mammon (Matt. 6:24). What also needs stressing is that such anxiously divided service, prompted by worry over our material well-being, is simply not necessary (Matt. 6:25-33). God understands all our needs, and he has uttered the strong and oathlike promise: **I will never fail you nor forsake you.** To that assurance the faithful respond in the words of Psalm 118:

> **The Lord is my helper,**
> **I will not be afraid;**
> **what can man do to me?**

Here again there surfaces the conviction that earthly realities are no security at all, and that having God is quite simply enough.

The Same Forever (13:7-8)

13:7—So far in the chapter nothing seems particularly closely related to the great themes of Hebrews, but at this point we begin to make contact again with central motifs: the word of God, faith as unwavering fidelity, the enduring and eternal status of Jesus Christ, and imagery associated with worship. But unfamiliar phrases also appear: **strange teachings** (v. 9), **foods** (v. 9), a Christian **altar** (v. 10), **outside the camp** (v. 11, 13), and **outside the gate** (v. 12).

This central section of the chapter opens and closes with a reference to **leaders** of the community. The readers are called to **remember** and **imitate** them (v. 7) and to **obey** and **submit to them** (v. 17).

A triple description of the leaders stands here at the beginning: (1) They **spoke to you the Word of God** (cf. 2:1-4). (2) Some of them have died (those in 17 and 24 include the author and are very much alive), since it is possible to contemplate and **consider the outcome of their life.** (3) Their lives were a case study in fidelity, a steady loyalty to Jesus, to the

Word of God, to unseen realities of the heavenly world, and readers should **imitate their faith.**

Those leaders, known to the community, continued into recent days the exemplary constancy of the older heroes of faith named in Chapter 11. In their unswerving loyalty all the way to the end, those leaders are models for the community to **remember, consider,** and **imitate.** The theme of imitation raised its head back in 6:12, where readers were summoned to overcome their sluggishness by becoming "imitators of those who through faith and patience inherit the promises." Indeed, imitation of leaders is a familiar theme in early Christianity (cf. Phil. 3:17; 1 Thess. 1:6).

13:8—The imperatives of verse 7 are not merely followed but undergirded by the great declaration of verse 8. Prophets, heroes, and leaders come and go, but **Jesus Christ is the same yesterday and today and for ever.**

Similar is the formula of Revelation that Jesus is the Alpha and the Omega (Rev. 1:17-18; 2:8; 22:13), but that sentence expresses primarily Jesus' power over all our beginnings and endings, over the beginning and end of the whole world, over empires and rulers of earth with all their pretensions and arrogance. Kingdoms rise and kingdoms fall, he was there in the beginning and will conquer in the end.

Hebrews confronts a different issue. Much in our world seem seductively stable, enduring, and trustworthy. But it is the grossest of errors to construct life on the quicksand of what this world calls secure. The apparently durable things of the world are sands in the hourglass and are in the process of passing away. Only God is unchanged and unchangeable, constant and reliable (James 1:2-28).

From first to last Hebrews stresses that Jesus is exalted at God's right hand, above all change and decay, impervious to the universal law of passing away (1:10-12). His throne is forever (1:8); he remains (1:11); when all things change he is still **the same** and his years will never end (1:12); his priesthood is permanent, enduring forever (7:24); he is perfect forever (7:28); and he gives to his own people access to unseen realities, to permanence, to the heavenly world.

Here We Have No Lasting City (13:9-16)

13:9—Do not be led away has been more colorfully rendered, "Do not be swept off your course" (NEB).[95] The community is in danger of being carried away by a flood if it should slip its anchor, its grip on Christ, through whom alone it enjoys a firm linkage to the stable world of God (2:1; 6:19; cf. 3:12; 10:35).

The danger is posed by **diverse and strange teachings.** That word **diverse** echoes the first words of the entire book. The multiplicity and varieties of ancient prophetic communications stand there in telling contrast to the singularity of God's speech in one who is Son. So here near the end the Word of God or message of Jesus Christ shines in the utter simplicity of its unity and integrity in opposition to **diverse teachings.**

That the teachings are plural and diversified indicates their fatal connection to the world of materiality and earthiness, of transiency and multiplicity, far removed from the heavenly world of permanence and simplicity.

Furthermore, those teachings were not held by faithful leaders now dead, but are marked as **strange** and foreign to the confession and tradition of faith (cf. 2 John 9; John 21:24).

The appeal is grounded in the statement that, after all, **it is well that the heart be strengthened by grace, not by foods.** Many have welcomed this addition as a key to understanding the chief issue in this difficult final chapter. The false teachings must revolve around foods, they say, and foods should be interpreted as in other and more familiar contexts. So it has been suggested that the community was embroiled in controversy (1) about food offered to pagan idols (1 Cor. 8–10), (2) about the usefulness or vanity of ascetic practices as assistance in achieving holiness (1 Tim. 4:3), (3) about the advisability of Gentile Christian observance of Jewish ritual food laws (Romans 14; Col. 2:16-23), or even (4) about the benefits of eating and drinking the Lord's Supper (John 6:60-63).

However, Jewish food laws were familiar and not **strange,** and elsewhere in Hebrews not one of these other ideas plays any role. What Hebrews everywhere does is to contrast the visible and the invisible, the earthly and the heavenly. Here **foods** stands opposite **grace.** Only the latter can really **strengthen hearts.** The former **have not benefited their adherents.**

It is nothing new for the author to be commending that which makes strong, steadfast, or stable (3:6, 14; 6:19) and that which genuinely benefits (4:2; 7:18). In impressive fashion he has previously exposed the inadequacies of the Levitical sacrificial system. That system, since it majors in a visible sanctuary and in tangible items like foods, drinks, and washings, is merely one more instance of the larger class of what he has called fleshly regulations (9:10). And it is that larger system or class of regulations with its attendant teachings and patterns of behavior, whether Levitical or pagan, which really captures his attention and arouses his concern.

Any system of fleshly regulations belongs to the earth. At best it can purify the flesh (9:13), but it is inherently incapable of purifying or perfecting the conscience (9:14, 9). That amounts to saying it can never "strengthen the heart" (13:9).

Warning is directed not against sacramentalistic tendencies in the church, nor against Jewish customs or foods offered to pagan idols, nor against abstemiousness or ascetic discipline flowering on spiritualizing or gnosticizing soil. The danger is broader: entrapment by worldly and fleshly concerns. Esau, for example, is held up as a negative model: food enticed him to peddle his birthright (12:16). Christians must beware lest they imitate him. They must rather follow those who faithfully turned their faces from earthly securities and fixed their eyes and their hearts on things unseen (11:7, 10, 14).

13:10—Liturgical rhetoric continues, as the author asserts **We have an altar.** This parallels his earlier statements that he and his readers "have" a high priest (4:14; 8:1). It is because their high priest has obtained a ministry in heaven, the true sanctuary or tabernacle, that they can be said to **have an altar.**

The second half of the verse is a bit more obscure than the first. Two interpretations (at least!) are possible. One begins by taking both the **altar** and the **tent** as heavenly realities. The other depends on understanding the **altar** as heavenly and the **tent** as earthly and inferior.

According to the first interpretation, the author and readers have a heavenly altar, and all those Christians who with them **serve the tent,** namely the heavenly sanctuary, have neither the right nor the need to eat the foods mentioned in verse 9.

An alternative interpretation is that non-Christians are the ones who **have no right to eat**—in the sense of receiving spiritual sustenance—from the Christian altar in heaven. The non-Christians do not benefit from the sacrifice consummated upon that heavenly altar. Disqualified are all **those who serve the tent,** namely the earthly tent with its fleshly regulations.

It is easy to exaggerate the differences in these possibilities. In either case the eyes and hearts of Christians are lifted heavenward to eternal and enduring realities altogether beyond the tangible and sensible. Their spiritual lives are not strengthened by any foods from any earthly altars. The author continues in the immediately following verses by asserting that the death of Jesus is like the sacrifices of the Day of Atonement, which were too holy to be eaten. We have spiritual sacrifices to be spiritually appropriated and enjoyed.

From an early date it came as a surprise and puzzle that Christians possessed neither sanctuary nor sacrifice, and the suspicion easily arose that they therefore also had no God and no real religion (see Irenaeus, *Against Heresies,* 4:17f). The author insists that Christians do have a spiritual religion with a great spiritual sacrifice to end all sacrifices, and benefits accrue to worshipers, but not through any material cult no matter how impressive, nor through visible ceremonies no matter how splendid, nor through any tangible foods from earthly altars no matter how sweet the savor they exude.

13:11—The assertions of verses 9-10 receive support from a pair of declarations. The first is drawn from Lev. 16:26: **For**

the bodies of those animals whose blood is brought into the sanctuary by the high priest as a sacrifice for sin are burned outside the camp.

Priests and worshipers regularly ate sacrificial grains and meats together, but the animals slaughtered on the Day of Atonement were extraordinary. Their **blood is brought into the sanctuary by the high priest,** ritually manipulated inside the Holy of Holies, the inner sanctum, one day a year, and so those particular animal sacrifices were uniquely sacred, exceptionally powerful, and dangerous. Precisely because those sacrifices were so holy and potent, **the bodies of those animals . . . are burned outside the camp.** It was forbidden to eat even the tiniest portion of the bullock and goat offered for the sins of the people on that day. No one, neither priest nor people, had "the right to eat" (v. 10) of those sacrifices.

13:12—The second declaration very nearly parallels the first: **So Jesus also suffered outside the gate in order to consecrate the people through his own blood.**

Here in one of a handful of references in Hebrews to an event in Jesus' earthly life (cf. 5:7; 7:14), we are reminded that Jesus died, quite literally and geographically, outside the city of Jerusalem, **outside the gate** (see John 19:20).

So Jesus' death outside the gate was foreshadowed in ancient sacrifices outside the camp on the annual Day of Atonement. Instead of being eaten, those sacrificial offerings were consumed utterly by fire, and their smoke and savor ascended to heaven. As the final atoning sacrifice, Jesus rose to heaven and left nothing on earth to be eaten. Indeed the new Christian worship is far superior both to the ancient Levitical shadow and to all pagan rites, outstripping them in sublimity and finely sweeping aside as crass, dull, and hopelessly earthbound all physical eating and drinking as a means of purifying the conscience or strengthening the heart (cf. John 4:21-24).

It is easy enough to follow the author when he talks about "the tent" as the earthly sanctuary of the old covenant and about "the camp" as the habitat of the Israelites in the wilderness. It is not difficult to follow him as he parallels the camp of the Israelites and the first century city of Jerusalem where Jesus was condemned to die. But all the time he is thinking of "tent" and "camp" also at a highly rarefied level. "The tent" can be the present evil age (9:9) and "the camp" is the world of visible, tangible, transient existence. And our true sanctuary and abiding city are above or as yet to come.[96]

The true tent or sanctuary is heavenly, set up not by any human hand but by the Lord. Christ is priest in that sanctuary. That he **suffered outside the gate** means that he despised earthly securities. He accepted crucifixion and at the cross stepped through the veil of his flesh. By means of death he moved beyond the whole realm of things earthly and penetrated into the most sacred environs of the heavenly sanctuary. He suffered thus **in order to sanctify the people through his own blood,** to wash them and qualify them for life by the power of his own sacrificed life.

His death was an event in two spheres: on earth and in heaven. Viewed as entrance into the heavenly sanctuary, his death is no mean miscarriage of justice, not the mere sad issue of human ignorance or malice. It is a sublime "sacrifice for sin" (v. 11) and an act of purification opening the way to the throne of grace (v. 12; cf. 1:3; 10:29).

13:13—The author calls us to forget about eating foods as a spiritual exercise. **Let us go forth to him outside the camp.** He summons us to follow Jesus on his upward and forward way, to make progress in our pilgrimage and press beyond the physical and visible world, careless of earthly sanctions and securities. The pilgrim may indeed **bear abuse** by being found in his disreputable company. Moses was willing (11:25-27). Jesus himself ignored the shame (12:2).

13:14—In this world of earth and matter, time and flux, **we have no lasting city.** Jesus looked up and looked ahead to "the joy" (12:2), and Hebrews speaks wonderfully of the quest for **the city which is to come** (cf. 11:10, 16), a better homeland

(11:16), a heavenly Jerusalem (12:22), an unshakable kingdom (12:27-28). All these are identical with the promised "rest" (Chaps. 2–4). Everything in the world is unstable, but the promised heavenly reward is immutable (cf. 1 Peter 1:4).

13:15—The sublimity of the promise evokes the challenge to offer up appropriate sacrifices. Spiritual sacrifices for a spiritual worship! Through Jesus our priest, then, **let us continually offer up a sacrifice of praise to God.** The Lord seeks not the blood of animals poured on altars or the smoke of their burning carcasses, not the observance of fleshly regulations, but **the fruit of lips that acknowledge his name** (cf. Hos. 14:2). This spiritual worship is not regulated by some festal calendar to be offered at scrupulously calculated intervals in the day or year. We are to offer this worship **continually,** as prayer never ceases and as songs rise from all the heart for all things, and at all times giving thanks (cf. Phil. 4:4; Eph. 5:19-20). To **acknowledge his name** means to recognize his character as creator and redeemer and to subject our lives to his authority.

13:16—This paragraph (vv. 7-16), with its argument about tents, altars, and sacrifices, seemed at first unconnected with the preceding (vv. 1-6). But now we are back to the virtues featured at the start of the chapter. God desires that his people at their "altar" (v. 10) offer him this sacrifice: **do not neglect to do good and to share what you have.** This is one of three great New Testament definitions of religion (cf. Rom. 12:1-3; James 1:27). So it appears that reciprocal love, hospitality, compassion, chastity, and contentment (13:1-6) are **sacrifices pleasing to God** (cf. 1 Peter 2:5).

Obey Your Leaders (13:17)
13:17—The author has summoned the community to **remember** and **imitate** faithful leaders now dead (v. 7), but now he exhorts, **obey your** living **leaders and submit to them** (cf. v. 24). Among these latter he numbers himself.

How was the community organized? **Leaders** is a general

word, like "officers." It does not specify the exact rank or function (cf. Acts 15:22).[97] Absent from Hebrews are any of the
familiar early Christian words for officer such as bishop, dea-
con, elder, evangelist, or apostle. But the **leaders** are described
as faithfully speaking the word of God (v. 7), a matter of highest importance to the author, **and they are keeping watch over**
the **souls** of the members and exercising vigilance on their
behalf. Like all guardians or shepherds they **will have to give
an account,** for they labor not autonomously but on behalf of
their Lord. The author speaks wooingly of joyful collabora-
tion in the community between the leaders and the led.

The material on the heavenly altar and the spiritual life
(13:8-16) is bracketed by references to leaders past (v. 7) and
present (v. 17).

■ Epistolary Ending: Blessings and Personal Greetings (13:18-25)

Pray for Us (13:18-19)

13:18-19—The writer is apparently one of the leaders and
seeks the prayers of the community, as Paul often sought the
intercessions of his congregations (1 Thess. 5:25; 2 Thess. 3:1;
Rom. 15:30). He asks for their prayers in connection with
talk of conscience and being restored. Leader and community
had apparently argued and had a falling out. Obedience (v. 17)
had been replaced by willfulness, rebellion, and separation.
He strongly asserts that he has a **clear conscience.** If he has
hurt them, they must know that it was inadvertently, for his
desire has always been to act **honorably in all things.** When
they begin again to pray for him, the bonds that had been
severed will begin to mend and he will **be restored to** them.

The Great Shepherd of the Sheep (13:20-21)

13:20-21—Mutual prayer binds heart to heart across vast
distances, and the writer not only seeks their prayers but
utters his on their behalf.

He invokes **the God of peace,** a favorite early Christian designation for God, as its repeated use by Paul testifies (1 Thess. 5:23; 2 Cor. 13:11; Phil. 4:9; Rom. 15:33; 16:20). The author has previously shown how Melchizedek resembles the Son of God and interpreted king of Salem to mean "king of Peace" (7:2). God and the Son of God, by conquering death and the devil (2:14), are the architects of ultimate and perfect peace.

God established peace when he **brought again from the dead our Lord Jesus.** God did something more and greater than simply restore him to the earth again, where life is governed by the universal law of transiency. Rather God literally "led him upward out of death," snatched him out of the thrall of death to the heights of exalted existence with himself.[98]

Here, as everywhere in Hebrews, what is stressed is not a resuscitation but exaltation to God's right hand (1:3, 13; 4:14; 7:26; 8:1; 10:12). The precise phrasing is drawn from the Greek version of Isa. 63:11. There the prophet speaks of God's rescue of his people through Moses at the Red Sea: "Where is he who brought up out of the sea the shepherd of his flock?"

God has brought up not just Moses but Jesus, not merely from the Red Sea but out of death itself, and he has exalted Jesus, not for his own sake, but for the sake of all God's people. Therefore Jesus is here called **the great shepherd of the sheep.** The church has many leaders past and present (vv. 7, 17), many shepherds (Eph. 4:11; 1 Peter 1:25; cf. Acts 20:28), but they serve under the one **shepherd** who, because of his uniqueness among all over all the rest, is simply designated **great** (cf. 4:14; 10:21). He is great, and he has great, high benefits to bestow.

As good shepherd he took responsibility for the whole flock of God and freely gave his life for them (John 10:11, 15-18). That outpoured life was not in vain. God led him up from the dead with that proffered **blood,** and it has become the means by which a new covenant has come into being in accord with the promise (Zech. 9:11; Isa. 55:3; Ezek. 37:26; Heb. 9:20;

12:24). This new **covenant** is **eternal**, as the redemption it brings is unchanging and unchangeable, as the priesthood of Christ is for ever (cf. 7:17, 21, 22; 9:12).

The author then focuses the entire tremendous weight of God's action in the oblation and exaltation of Jesus. He prays that God may **equip you with everything good that you may do his will.** From the beginning the author has been spelling out the good things Jesus is and the good things God has done through him. Through him the community has been purified from the stain of sin, delivered from the old bondage to death, perfected and granted access to the throne of grace. Through him in the present and the future God continues to **equip** and he keeps on **working in you that which is pleasing in his sight.** Lives of fidelity and of doing his will, as described in 13:1-6, are the liturgy and sacrifice genuinely **pleasing in his sight, through Jesus Christ.**

Jesus is the same forever (v. 8), and the author seals his prayers with a solemn doxology: **To whom be glory for ever and ever! Amen.**

Bear with My Word of Exhortation (13:22-25)

13:22—From end to end Hebrews is, in the author's own vocabulary, a **word of exhortation,** a homily or edifying discourse aimed at transforming the readers' hearts and reforming their lives, not merely informing their minds, however artfully and intellectually challenging the work may be (cf. Acts 13:15; Heb. 12:5). Hebrews is a dazzling display of Greek rhetoric and substantial argument, but **exhortation,** encouragement, and moral appeal are at the core of the author's purpose.

The latter half of the verse could be rendered woodenly and literalistically: "I have epistled you briefly." [99] But has he really written so **briefly,** and is this work an epistle?

Some interpreters press both the "epistled" and the "briefly" and suggest that Hebrews originally ended at 12:29. Chapter 13 all by itself is the "brief epistle" attached as a covering letter designed to commend the preceding treatise. Still, it seems better to regard Chapter 13 as integral to the communication from the start, as has been done here.

But is this work brief? It is shorter than Romans and 1 Corinthians. But more relevant than such a comparison are the author's own declarations that he could have expounded in greater detail the furnishings of the Holy of Holies (9:5) and the exploits of individual heroes of faith (11:32). The work is long enough, and the author may be seeking the reader's indulgence with a conventional phrase about brevity.

13:23—The sole member of the Christian community to be named in all of Hebrews is **our brother Timothy.** The only **Timothy** known to us from other parts of the New Testament is Paul's younger colleague and companion (Acts 16:1-2), co-sender of several letters (2 Corinthians, Philippians, Colossians, 1 and 2 Thessalonians, and Philemon), and principal recipient of 1 and 2 Timothy.

Timothy has been released. That means he has either just been freed from prison or he has set out on a journey (cf. Acts 13:3; 28:25).[100] In either case the author anticipates Timothy's arrival and hopes to see the readers in company with Timothy at an early date.

13:24—The author of Hebrews composed his work not for any one group within the community, but for all of them as a complex whole consisting of **all your leaders and all the saints.** That last is a common early designation for the totality of Christian people and is especially relevant here at the close of a work which speaks everywhere of Jesus' work as a high priestly activity of sanctifying, consecrating, and purifying.

Who are **those who come from Italy** and who **send you greetings?** All that can be said is that the author is somehow associated with Christians from Italy (cf. Acts 2:10; 28:16; Romans) who join him in greeting the readers.

The work as a whole was intended to be read aloud in a gathering of the congregation. It would take about an hour to read it. And it closes appropriately with a final blessing: **Grace be with all of you. Amen.**

SELECTED BIBLIOGRAPHY

Bruce, F. F. *The Epistle to the Hebrews, The New International Commentary on the New Testament.* Grand Rapids: Wm. B. Eerdmans, 1964. Bruce thinks the recipients once held Jewish convictions of a nonconformist sort (similar to those of the Qumraners) and were in present danger of relaxing their Christian faith and hope and high morality. Commenting clearly and forcefully on the English text (American Standard Version), Bruce offers in his numerous footnotes a wealth of information on the vocabulary and syntax of the Greek original.

Buchanan, George Wesley. *To the Hebrews, The Anchor Bible.* Garden City: Doubleday, 1972. Notable for the effort to understand Hebrews as a homily on Psalm 110 by a scholar of the early Church, converted from Judaism, who practiced the kind of Jewish midrashic interpretation of Biblical material found in portions of the Dead Sea Scrolls, in parts of Philo, and among ancient rabbis.

Luther, Martin. *Lectures on Hebrews, Luther's Works.* Vol. 29. Saint Louis: Concordia Publishing House, 1968. Luther lectured on Hebrews from April 1517 till March 1518. In some respects the gathering storm of those fateful months seems distant from these pages with their calm consideration of the text and their scholarly dialogue with Jerome, Chrysostom, Augustine, Peter Lombard, Aquinas, Lyra, and Faber.

But it is intriguing to watch Luther's struggling to find fresh ways to express the wonder of God's speech in the Son and the answering miracle of human faith.

Moffatt, James. *The Epistle to the Hebrews, The International Critical Commentary.* Edinburgh: T. & T. Clark, 1924. A masterful commentary, written with verve and grace, by a scholar who continually illumines the Greek text, sensitive to all its nuances and subtleties, and lays bare its solid links with a broad range of classical and hellenistic Greek authors.

Pfitzner, Victor C. *Hebrews, Chi Rho Commentary.* Adelaide: Lutheran Publishing House, 1978. A commentary on the English text (RSV) of Hebrews remarkable for the extent to which it combines solid interpretation, edification, and readability.

Thompson, James W. *The Beginnings of Christian Philosophy: The Epistle to the Hebrews.* Washington, D.C.: The Catholic Biblical Association of America, 1982. Not a commentary but a set of essays on central themes and passages in Hebrews, arguing that the author of Hebrews stands in the tradition of Plato (Middle Platonism) and thinks primarily not in terms of apocalyptic or eschatology but in terms of the contrast between the stable and unchanging world above and the world of flux here below.

NOTES

1. Reginald H. Fuller, "The Letter to the Hebrews," in Gerhard Krodel, ed., *Hebrews, James, 1 and 2 Peter, Jude, Revelation* (Philadelphia: Fortress Press, 1977).
2. See James Moffatt, *A Critical and Exegetical Commentary on the Epistle to the Hebrews* (Edinburgh: T. & T. Clark, 1924), pp. LVI-LXIV. See also Nigel Turner, *A Grammar of New Testament Greek*, vol. 4: *Style* (Edinburgh: T. & T. Clark), 4:106-113.
3. Eusebius, *Ecclesiastical History* VI, 25.
4. F. W. Danker, in his brief commentary on Hebrews in *Invitation to the New Testament Epistles IV* (Garden City: Image Books, 1980), consistently uses the feminine pronouns *she* and *her* of the author. The document is anonymous, so a choice must be made almost arbitrarily; Danker thinks it will be efficacious for male readers to experience something of the jolt to which female readers are routinely subjected.
5. Others find the dualism to be Gnostic. See Ernst Käsemann, *Das wandernde Gottesvolk*, 4th ed. (Göttingen: Vandenhoeck und Ruprecht, 1961). Werner Georg Kümmel, *Introduction to the New Testament, rev. ed.* (Nashville: Abingdon Press, 1975); Helmut Koester, *Introduction to the New Testament* (Philadelphia: Fortress Press, 1982), 2:272-6.
6. In some circles Abraham was viewed as the heir appointed by God (Heb. 11:9-16), but Christians modified those traditions and viewed Jesus as the singular seed of Abraham and declared that all those who are children of God by faith in Jesus Christ are the descendants of Abraham and heirs. See Jubilees 17:3; cf. 22:14; Sirach 44:21; Rom. 4:13; Gal. 3:29.
7. Acccording to Heb. 1:3, the Son is *apaugasma* ("effulgence" or "radiance") of God's glory, a stream of light issuing from the source of light and substantially identical to the source. And the Son is *charaktēr* ("impress" or "exact replica") of God's hypostasis ("nature"). The unknown Alexandrian author of the Wisdom of Solomon (latter half of the first century B.C.) wrote similarly of Divine Wisdom (*Sophia*): "She is a breath of the power of God, and a pure emanation (*apaugasma*) of

the glory of the Almighty . . . She is a reflection of the eternal light, a spotless mirror of the workings of God, and an image (*eikōn*, synonym of *charaktēr*) of his goodness" (Wisd. of Sol. 7:25-26). Philo used similar language of the Word of God (*Logos: On the Creation* 146; *On Noah's Work as a Planter* 18; cf. *The Special Laws* 4:123).

8. Our author says that the Son bears (*pherō*) the world by his powerful Word. Philo calls the Word of the eternal God the sure prop of the universe. No material thing is strong enough to bear the weight (*achtho-phorein*) of the world: *On Noah's Work as a Planter* 8; in *Who Is the Heir* 36, Philo uses *pherō* to mean "give life" or "bring into being" (cf. *On the Change of Names* 192). Moffatt notes that Philo wrote of the logos as the pilot and guide of the universe (*On the Migration of Abraham* 6) and Chrysostom took it the same way.

9. On Psalm 110 in early Christianity see David M. Hay, *Glory at the Right Hand* (Nashville: Abingdon, 1973).

10. Among the "elementary doctrines of Christ" is the resurrection of the dead" (6:1-2). Compare also 11:19 and 35, and see the discussion of 13:20.

11. A number of people have suggested that Hebrews closely resembles Colossians in the way both documents oppose a false estimate of the status and function of angels: F. D. V. Narborough, *The Epistle to the Hebrews in the Revised Version* (Oxford: Clarendon Press, 1930); Günther Bornkamm, "Das Bekenntnis im Hebräerbrief," *Theologische Blätter* 21 (1942), reprinted in *Studien zur Antike und Urchristentum* (München: Christian Kaiser Verlag, 1959), pp. 188-203; T. W. Manson, "The Problem of the Epistle to the Hebrews," *Bulletin of the John Rylands Library* 32 (1949), reprinted in *Studies in the Gospels and Epistles*, ed. Matthew Black (Manchester: Manchester University Press, 1962), pp. 242-258.

The possible connections between Hebrews and Colossians featuring a false teaching about angelic beings have been greatly developed by Charles P. Anderson, "The Epistle to the Hebrews and the Pauline Letter Collection," *HTR* 59 (1966):429-38; "Who Wrote 'The Epistle from Laodicea'?", *JBL* 85 (1966):436-40; "Hebrews among the Letters of Paul," *Studies in Religion* 5(1975-6):258-66. And see Robert Jewett, "Hebrews and the Lycus Valley Controversy" (Paper presented to the Annual Meeting of the Society of Biblical Literature, New York, October, 1970), and *Letter to Pilgrims* (New York: The Pilgrim Press, 1981), pp. 5-13.

12. Babylonian Talmud, Hagigah 14a.

13. The "comrades" or "companions" (*metochoi*) of the king in Psalm 45 were perhaps other kings invited to the royal wedding. But our author takes the psalm as a prophecy of the Messiah and pictures the angels as his comrades or courtiers. The word *metochoi* is used of believers as "sharers" in a heavenly calling (3:1), in the Holy Spirit (6:4), and in the Lord's discipline (12:8). At 3:14 our author calls the community *metochoi tou Christou*, which may be translated either "sharers in Christ" or "companions of Christ."

14. *pararreō* means to "flow by" or "be washed away," *BAGD*.

15. On angels as mediators of the Law see Gal. 3:19; Acts 7:38, 53; Deut. 33:2; Psalm 68:17; Jos. *Ant.* 15. 136.

16. Words formed from the root *bebai* occur seven (or eight) times in Hebrews: A "valid" message (2:2); the Christian message "confirmed, attested, or guaranteed" (2:3); hold our confidence "firm" to the end (3:14, also 3:6 in some ancient manuscripts); an oath as "confirmation" (6:16); a "steadfast" anchor (6:19); a will becomes "effective" or "valid" at death (9:17); hearts "strengthened" or "confirmed" (13:9).

    The author offers many synonyms for the same idea, and loves to speak of the certainty, reliability, eternity, and unshakable character of the heavenly realities.

17. The word *ameleō* means to "neglect" or "care nothing about" something (*BAGD*). See Heb. 8:9 (Jer. 38:32); Matt. 22:5; 1 Tim. 4:14; Wisd of Sol. 3:10; 2 Macc. 4:14.

18. The present passage has a Trinitarian cast, speaking as it does of the Lord (Jesus), God (the Father), and the Holy Spirit. Our author speaks most characteristically of the Spirit as the inspirer of Holy Scripture: 3:7; 9:8; 10:15. Elsewhere (6:4) he calls the readers "partakers" (*metochoi*, note 13) of the Holy Spirit, declares that Christ offered himself through the eternal spirit (9:14), and warns that deliberate sin outrages "the Spirit of grace" (10:29).

19. Whatever relationship our author may have had with the Platonism of his age, he is of course thoroughly un-Platonic and un-Philonic in insisting on the greatness of what Jesus has accomplished in his flesh in the material world at the cross.

20. In different contexts the Greek word *brachy*, here translated "for a little while lower," can mean a short space (Acts 27:28), a small quantity (John 6:7), or a short time (Heb. 2:7; cf. Isa. 57:17); see *BAGD*.

21. Luther unfortunately followed Chrysostom in thinking of a mere "tasting" as echoing the "little while" of 2:7, 9. Tasted, they thought, meant that he spent only a short time in death and was then quickly resurrected. But the thrust of the passage and the normal usage of the phrase indicates that the author meant that Jesus fully and deeply experienced death. See Moffatt's commentary and Johannes Behm, *TDNT* 1:677.

22. On *archēgos* see Gerhard Delling *TDNT* 1:487-8; *BAGD*.

23. Most important for an understanding of the family of words meaning "perfection," "perfected," or "make perfect" in Hebrews *(teleios, teleiotēs, teleioō, teleiōsis, teleiōtēs, teleō, telos)* are Lala Kalyan Kumar Dey, *The Intermediary World and Patterns of Perfection in Philo and Hebrews* (Missoula: Scholars Press, 1975) and Gerhard Delling, *TDNT* 8:49-87. See also Paul Johannes DuPlessis, *TELEIOS: The Idea of Perfection in the New Testament* (Kampen: Kok, 1959); A. Wikgren, "Patterns of Perfection in the Epistle to the Hebrews," *NTS* 6 (1960):159-67 and *BAGD*.

24. In his commentary on Heb. 1:2 Martin Luther wrote that the humanity of Christ is "the holy ladder" by which we ascend to the love and knowledge of God.

    Kenneth Hagen, *A Theology of Testament in the Young Luther: The Lectures on Hebrews* (Leiden: E. J. Brill, 1974), discusses the significance of Luther's lectures on Hebrews in 1517-1518, noting how Luther in his exegesis stressed the righteousness of God, Scripture as promise, God's covenant, and faith as trust and certitude. Hagen subsequently reviewed the treatment of Hebrews in 16th century exegesis after Luther in his *Hebrews Commenting from Erasmus to Beze, 1516-1598* (Tübingen: J. C. B. Mohr, 1981). Luther's Lectures on Hebrews are readily available in volume 29 of the American Edition of *Luther's Works.*

25. *Epilambanomai* is the word in 2:16. It means to grasp for oneself, to bring into one's sphere or fellowship, to take someone's hand in order to help. See Luke 14:4 on Jesus' healing hand and see 20:20, 26 for the use of the term in a negative sense. Gerhard Delling *TDNT* 4:9. *Boētheō* in 2:18 means "help" or "furnish aid." On both words see also *BAGD*.

26. The Greek word is *homologia* (3:1; 4:14; 10:23). The verb *homologeō* occurs in 11:13 and 13:15. See Otto Michel, *TDNT* 5:207-217.

27. Philo speaks of God's dwelling in heaven, in the whole universe, and in the soul. One must go forth from the house

of the senses in order to return home to God. Only thus can the soul fulfil its destiny or calling to be God's house, his holy temple *(On Dreams* 1:149). Hebrews says that people become God's house by heeding the heavenly call (3:1) and by retaining their bold confidence in their hope (3:6).

28. *Katechō* (3:6, 14; 10:23) and *kratein* (4:4; 6:18) are especially significant terms in Hebrews. The readers were in danger of being swayed from that which is stable and enduring, of losing their grip on abiding realities. Therefore the author calls them to "grasp" and "hold fast" things unseen which alone are immutable. "Faith" in Hebrews is just such a grasping and holding. On *katechō* see Hermann Hanse, *TDNT* 2:829-30.

29. *Parrēsia* and *kauchēma* are the words translated in the RSV as "confidence" and "pride." TEV translates the pairs as "courage and confidence." Classically *parrēsia* denoted the speech of the free citizen of the polis who had the privilege of "saying everything" (pas-rhēsis), unlike slaves or aliens who were constrained to hold back their words or utter them only in private or on the sly. Philo characterizes all the wise *(sophoi)* as friends *(philoi)* of God and remarks that frankness in speech *(parrēsia)* is a sign of friendship. In Philo, as in Hebrews (4:16; 10:19, 35), *parrēsia* designates a bold approach to God. Moses, as a friend of God (Exod. 33:11), was able to approach God directly, without wavering, and speak with God, not in presumption, but in the benign audacity of friendship *(Who Is the Heir* 21; cf. Heinrich Schlier, *TDNT* 5:871-86). In the Gospel of John *parrēsia* calls attention to the public teaching of Jesus, while in Acts the Spirit bestows the gift of *parrēsia* for the sake of courageous proclamation.

   Kauchēma ("pride" or "boast") is here a synonym for *parrēsia*. In Philo the boast *(auchēma)* of the soul is in its ability to soar above the created world, pass beyond its boundaries, and hold fast to the uncreated alone *(The Preliminary Studies* 131-4; see also L. L. K. Dey, *Patterns of Perfection,* p. 197, and J. W. Thompson, *The Beginnings of Christian Philosophy* (Washington: Catholic Biblical Association), pp. 92-94.

30. *(metochoi).* See note 13.

31. *Hysterein* ("fail to reach" or "be excluded," cf. Rom. 3:23, cf. 12:15) is the opposite of "enter" (3:19). The same word is used in 11:37 of righteous sufferers to describe them as being "destitute," that is, being people who through no fault of their own are lacking.

32. *(Pistis):* 4:2; 6:1, 12; 10:22, 38, 39; 12:2; 13:7. It occurs 24 times in Chapter 11. *Pistos,* "faithful," occurs in 2:17; 3:2, 5; 10:23; 11:11. *Pisteuō* is used only in 4:3 ("believing people") and 11:6 ("believe"). See note 66.

33. *Sabbatismos,* "sabbath rest," is our author's coinage. *Katapausis* is "rest" in 3:11, 18; 4:1, 3 (twice), 5, 10, 11.

    Buchanan interprets the "rest" and all its many synonyms in Hebrews—the world to come, a heavenly country, the future city—to mean a heritage not located in heaven but situated firmly upon the earth. He thinks the author and his community expected to inhabit the promised land of Canaan under the rule of the Messiah. Most interpreters read Hebrews differently and think "rest" refers to a future heavenly or transcendent reality.

    In the Old Testament and Judasim, "rest" came to be used as another word for salvation. In Jewish apocalyptic (4 Ezra), "rest" means the new future world which will replace the present world.

    In the two Alexandrians, Philo and Clement, "rest" is associated with God just as tranquility, stability, and immortality also are his, while movement and change characterize the material world.

    In Gnosticism, "rest" was often used as a name for God or for the original home of the Gnostic, who wanders homeless and experiences only unrest in the material world.

    The discussion in Hebrews 3–4 shows that rest *(katapausis)* and sabbath rest *(sabbatismos)* both mean entrance into the presence of God, attaining access to the homeland (11:11, 14), the city with foundations (11:10, 16; 12:22; 13:14), the unshakable kingdom (12:28).

    On 3:11; 11:10-16; 12:22; 13:14 see George Wesley Buchanan, *To the Hebrews* (Garden City: Doubleday, 1972). Especially important is J. W. Thompson, *Beginnings,* pp. 81-102. See also Otto Bauernfeind, "Katapausis," *TDNT* 3:627-8, and Edvard Lohse, "Sabbatismos," *TDNT* 7:34-5.

34. *Tetrachēlismena* is the perfect passive participle of *trachēlizō.* The cognate noun *trachēlos* means neck or throat. The verb means to expose and lay bare the throat or neck.

35. *(proserchomai):* 4:16; 7:25; 10:1, 22; 11:6; 12:18, 22. The English word *proselyte* (meaning a "convert") is derived from the perfect tense of *proserchomai* (see *proselēlythate* in 12:18, 22). A proselyte is one who "comes to" a new faith or

"approaches" God out of a background of unbelief. The word originally meant "to devote or apply oneself to." Besides numerous ordinary secular meanings ("to have dealings with someone" or "to take up an enterprise or project"), the word was commonly used in the Greek Old Testament (LXX) in a cultic sense meaning to come to God in sacrifice, worship, or prayer. It is used also of a respectful approach to wisdom (Sirach 4:15; 24:19). See Johannes Schneider, *TDNT* 2:683-4.

36. For a recent German discussion of this hymn, see Otto Michel, *Der Brief an die Hebraer* (Göttingen: Vandenhoeck & Ruprecht, 1975), pp. 219-229. For a discussion in English, see David M. Stanley, *Jesus in Gethsemane* (New York: Paulist, 1980), pp. 99-104.

37. *Agōnia* is the English "agony" (Luke 22:14). *Agōn*, a cognate, is "an athletic contest" or "struggle" (Heb. 12:1). See commentary on 12:1.

38. Behind "offered up" is *prosenegkas* (from *prospherō*). The verb is commonly used of offering gifts (Matt. 2:11) or sacrifices (Matt. 5:23-4; Heb. 5:1, 3; 8:3-4; 9:7, 9; 10:1, 2; 11:17). In Heb. 7:27 (variant reading; the text has *anapherō*) and 9:14, 25, cf. 28, it is used of Jesus' self-offering. Did the author think of Jesus' offerings of prayers and petitions (5:7) as a priestly activity in contrast to that of Aaron (5:1)? F. F. Bruce, with reference to A. B. Bruce, *The Humiliation of Christ* (1895), denies it. Moffatt thinks that *prospherō* in 5:7 is a subconscious echo of the same word in 5:1-3. Our author thinks in terms of one single offering of self on the part of Jesus, not something repeated during his ministry or continued in the heavenly sanctuary. See commentary on 7:25; 9:28. On *prospherō* see Konrad Weiss, *TDNT* 9:67, who takes the word in a cultic sense everywhere in Hebrews, including 5:7.

39. *(emathen/epathen)*. The words appear paired also in other forms, for example, *pathei/mathei*—"one learns by suffering." Aeschylus called it a law of Zeus that mortals should achieve wisdom through suffering. Prometheus learned from his suffering, and Herakles (Hercules) not only produced his labors, but his labors produced him.

Moffatt notes that in Greek authors, including Philo, the notion is almost always applied to stupid or thoughtless persons or to offenders and that the author of Hebrews is daring in applying to Jesus in his sinlessness an idea elsewhere nearly confined to the immature or undisciplined (cf. 12:5-11).

40. "Author of eternal salvation" is *aitios sōtērias aiōniou*. Philo calls Noah the author of his son Ham's salvation (*On the Virtues* 202) and designates the serpent as the author of complete salvation or deliverance for all who looked upon it (*On Husbandry* 96). Although the Red Sea was the instrument of death for the Egyptians, it was the source of salvation or preservation for Israel (*Contemplative Life* 86). God himself is the author of salvation for his people (*Special Laws* 1:252).

41. (*dys-ermēneutos*).

42. The same Greek word *nōthros* lies behind "dull" of hearing (5:11) and "sluggish" (6:12). On *nōthros* see Herbert Preisker, *TDNT* 4:1126.

43. Among other things, *ta stoicheia* are the letters of the alphabet, the elements from which the world is formed (earth, air, fire, water), and basic teachings or mere rudiments as opposed to advanced wisdom. See Gerhard Delling, *TDNT* 7:670-87 and *BAGD*.

44. Why is the higher teaching called "the word of righteousness"? In the immediate context "the word of righteousness" is described as a more difficult word than the first principles. It is hard to explain, solid food and not milk, intended not for infants but for the mature, who have their faculties trained by exercise to distinguish between good and evil. This last phrase should be compared with 12:11 where it is said that discipline (*paideia*) yields fruit rich in peace, namely righteousness, for those who have been trained by that discipline (cf. James 3:18).

     Just before his speaking about the word of righteousness the author has begun to describe Jesus as high priest forever (4:14–5:10), and he will return to that theme in 7:1 and speak immediately of Jesus' high priesthood as being of the same order as that of Melchizedek, whose name he interprets to mean "king of righteousness" and "king of peace." Jesus is the "king of righteousness" because he loves righteousness (1:9), indeed came precisely to do God's will (10:4-10), and by his priestly service purifies consciences (1:3; 9:14) and makes perfect, something which the old sacrifices were not able to do (10:1). Thus the "word of righteousness" is all about Jesus who loves righteousness and peace, and it is not apprehended by all.

     Gottlob Schrenk (*TDNT* 2:198) follows Riggenbach in taking the phrase to signify the correct speech of an adult as opposed to the babbling of an infant. Moffatt notes that interpretation of the phrase but rejects it in favor of what moderns would call "moral truth." The interpretation offered above is in line with Moffatt but moves beyond into a theological understanding of the phrase in line with the use of "righteousness" elsewhere in our author's document. Besides the commentaries, see John Reumann, *Righteousness in the New Testament* (Philadelphia and New York: Fortress and Paulist Presses, 1982), pp. 158-66.

45. *Teleios* is the Greek word translated "mature." See discussion on 2:10.

46. In describing two levels of learning, one of which is "milk" or "the ABCs" and the other of which is "solid food" or a word "hard to explain" (*dysermēneutos*), Hebrews both resembles and differs from the educational philosophies of Philo and other Hellenistic authors in the Platonic tradition. Plato and Platonists reflected on the uses of such subjects as astronomy, geometry, arithmetic, grammar, music, and gymnastics on the one hand, and of philosophy on the other. The subjects of the first level, fit for the child (*nēpios*), do not themselves produce virtue or wisdom but do represent a necessary preliminary stage preparing the mind to go further. From Plato to Epictetus, philosophy was the higher stage of education, reached only by discipline. In turn, only philosophy produced virtue and led the mind to God and thus to its goal (*telos*).

Athletic images typically and easily mingle with educational. When Heb. 5:14 says that exercise or practice (*hexis*) like that of the athlete (cf. 10:32; 12:1, 11) trains (*gymnazō*) the faculties, so that the person can progress from a childish to a mature (*teleios*) condition, it is still speaking the familiar language of Hellenistic pedagogy.

For Philo life is an athletic contest (*agōn*), and the wise person is one who, trained in the gymnastics of the soul, is able to finish the race and carry off the victor's prize. Spiritual conditioning includes not only instruction and practice, but also adversity, blows, and suffering. See note on 5:8-9.

Philo pictures Jacob as a (spiritually) trained athlete (*On Sobriety* 65; cf. *On Husbandry* 159-160). Indeed all Philo's scriptural heroes are portrayed as spiritual athletes.

See note 64. On all this see J. W. Thompson, "Hebrews 5:11-14 and Paideia," in *Beginnings of Christian Philosophy*, pp. 17-40; see also Victor C. Pfitzner, *Paul and the Agōn Motif* (Leiden: E. J. Brill, 1967).

47. Some have thought that Hebrews declares all postbaptismal sin to be unforgiveable. Tertullian in the third cenutry believed that the author was here condemning especially adultery and fornication. The author clearly distinguishes accidental and deliberate sins, condemning the latter.

    In his commentary on Hebrews, Luther does not display any uneasiness whatsoever with the assertion that there is no repentance for the lapsed. He understands the passage to be speaking, not about just any sin at all, but about falling into active unbelief and so imagining that one can be saved without Christ and his cross. What is impossible is to restore someone who has begun with Christ but who then later attaches himself to another. Later (at 10:26) Luther quotes with favor Chrysostom who commented that at 10:26 our author does not say that there is no further remission but that there is no second baptism and no second cross.

    Compare M. Yoma 8:9, "If a man said, 'I will sin and repent, and sin again and repent,' he will be given no chance to repent. If he said, 'I will sin and the Day of Atonement will effect atonement,' then the Day of Atonement effects no atonement."

48. *Makrothymia* is the noun. *Makrothymeō* is the verb in 6:15. See note. Luther wrote at 6:12 that "faith causes the heart to cling fast to celestial things and to be carried away and to dwell in things that are invisible."

49. According to Philo, the foolish are ruled by their unstable nature and are tossed about like ships caught in a storm, capable neither of smooth sailing nor of secure riding at anchor. God is unwaveringly stable, and nearness to God produces stability and quiet (*On the Posterity of Cain* 22-23).

50. Melchizedek is named in Hebrews 5:6, 10; 6:20; 7:1, 10, 11, 15, 17. Hebrews paraphrases or quotes absolutely everything written in the Old Testament about Melchizedek. Historically Melchizedek was a Canaanite priest-king, ruler of the city-state of Salem (Jerusalem?). As such he met Abraham returning from his successful surprise attack on the band of marauding kings who had sacked Sodom and captured Lot. He prepared a meal for Abraham, blessed him, and received tithes from him. That encounter with Abraham is reported in Gen. 14:18-20. Melchizedek is named within the Old Testament only once again, at Psalm 110:4, where the Israelite king is saluted with the words, "You are a priest forever after the order of Melchizedek." This solemn greeting hails the king,

God's adopted son (Ps. 2:7), not only as kingly source of righteousness and peace, but also as mediator between God and his people and hence as possessing a priestly function transcending that of the Levitical priesthood.

Ps. 110:4 itself is evidence that people had begun to meditate upon the figure of Melchizedek and that he had already achieved considerable stature.

The psalm was eagerly seized upon by the Hasmonean dynasty in the second century B.C. (some say it was written for the dynasty) and used by that priestly family to bolster their claims to royal prerogatives. They styled themselves and were accepted by many as a new class of priest-kings, successors to the leadership exercised by Moses and then by the Aaronic priests. They assumed the emblems of royalty and of high priesthood (1 Macc. 10:20-21), and individual rulers in the dynasty are designated by the Melchizedekian title "high priest forever" (1 Macc. 14:41) or "priests of the Most High God" (cf. Jubilees 32:1; Josephus, *Antiquities of the Jews.* 16:163; bRosh Hashanah 18b; Assumption of Moses 6:1).

A few fragments of a scroll naming Melchizedek were discovered in 1965 in cave 11 at Qumran, setting off a flurry of investigation, not only of that reconstructed column of ancient text, but also of the relations between the community at Qumran and the letter to the Hebrews. The document is a running commentary on a number of scriptural passages, chief of which is Isa. 61:1-2, on the theme of the coming time of salvation. Melchizedek is named several times. It is said that he brings in the year of the Lord's favor (Isa. 61:2), the year of Jubilee (Leviticus 25), the dawning of the time of salvation, of return for exiles, of liberty for captives, and of atonement for all the children of light. The fragmentary condition of the document makes it impossible to tell exactly how atonement occurs, but it comes as a result of Melchizedek's activity, and he is clearly pictured as standing as high priest in the presence of God.

The document quotes Ps. 82:1. It speaks of the heavenly one standing in the celestial assembly, judging among the heavenly ones or angels. That scene is then interpreted with the aid of Ps. 7:7-8, "God shall judge the nations," and Ps. 82:2, "How long will you accept the wicked?" and is taken to mean that Melchizedek will, with the help of good angels, wage successful warfare against Belial (Satan) and the evil spirits and rescue the children of light from their power. Then Isaiah's words extolling the beauty of the feet upon the mountains bearing good tidings of victory (Isa. 52:7; 61:1-2) will be actualized, and that heavenly one, Melchizedek, will be king. So Melchizedek will act as priest, working in the heavenly sanctuary, and as king, waging war on Belial and bringing salvation to God's people (cf. Testament of Levi 18:1– 19:2).

The Dead Sea Scroll 11Q Melchizedek has been interpreted in two differing ways. Most have followed the editor of the document in interpreting Melchizedek as a heavenly being and then in identifying him with the archangel Michael, who elsewhere in the scrolls is the Prince of Light (1 QM 13; 17:5-9; CDC 5:18) and Angel of Truth (1 QS 3:24; cf. Daniel 12) who wages war on Belial as stated in the preceding paragraphs.

In an alternative view, Melchizedek is not a heavenly being or angel but an historical figure within the Qumran community. He was seen by his comrades as embodying the characteristic features of the biblical Melchizedek. To them he was a "king of justice," a ruler or military leader in the community, and one who was expected to fulfill the role of Messiah and vindicate the chosen people.

Interpretations have differed and will continue to do so, partly because of the mutilated condition of the text. It is a single column reconstructed from 13 separate fragments, and there are numerous gaps in the text.

Philo notes that Melchizedek's priesthood is unique, not dependent upon any human tradition nor mediated through any human teacher. (Josephus says he built the first temple at Jerusalem and was the first priest to officiate there, *War* 6.438; *Antiquities* 1.180ff.). He was thus self-taught and independent and was identified by Philo as the Logos or Reason.

Philo offers etymologies of "Melchizedek" (i.e., King of of righteousness) and of "Salem" (i.e., peace) and ponders Melchizedek's offering to Abraham not water but wine (Gen. 14:18). The notion that Melchizedek is the righteous king of peace leads Philo to praise the peaceful influences of the truly royal mind. That he offered wine means that he brings spiritual intoxication by lifting the mind to God. As Logos, Melchizedek offers unmingled wine and is priestly mediator between God and humankind. (See *The Preliminary Studies* 99; *Allegorical Interpretation* 3.79-82.)

Hebrews fastens on the notion presented in Psalm 110 that Melchizedek belongs to a different "order" from Levitical or Aaronic priests. The psalm itself hints at the definition of that order by its talk about being a priest "for ever." "For ever" could mean that priestly prerogatives have shifted to a new dynasty of earthly priests and that the new family would enjoy priestly privileges perpetually and uninterruptedly.

Our author's expositions of the words "for ever" (6:20) and the additional word "remains" (*menei,* 7:3) indicates that he understands the Melchizedekian order in contrast to the Aaronic or Levitical, not in chronological or historical, but in spatial or philosophical terms.

Melchizedek belongs to the heavenly sphere, whose mark is eternity or indestructible life. Levitical or Aaronic priesthood is derivative, belonging to the material and physical world of change and decay, transience and death. Sacrificial acts performed in this sphere must be repeated and are never complete, perfect, or finished. Finality does not belong to the earth or to earthly sacrifices at earthly shrines.

Hebrews triumphantly declares that Jesus is priest for ever, that his priesthood endures, that he lives with the power of indestructible life, and that his sacrifice need not be repeated but is valid once for all, for everyone and forever, precisely because it has been offered in the heavenly rather than in the earthly sanctuary. In all of this, Hebrews is far closer to Philo than to the Dead Sea Scrolls in the portrait it offers of Melchizedek. Our author and Philo apparently breathe the same air, praising that which leads upward to God out of the world of sense and change. Theirs is not the rhetoric of apocalyptic visionaries.

Nevertheless, our author differs decisively from Philo, not only in calling Jesus a priest for ever after the order of Melchizedek, but especially in insisting that Jesus performed his priestly and mediatorial role, not by offering the high lessons of Reason or Logos nor by remaining aloof from passion, emotion, change, and suffering, but by becoming for a little while lower than the angels and by tasting death even in the shameful form of crucifixion (2:18; 5:8; 9:26; 13:12). See especially L. L. K. Dey, *Patterns of Perfection,* 185-214; J. W. Thompson, *Beginnings of Christian Philosophy,* "The Conceptual Background and Purpose of the Midrash in Hebrews 7," pages 116-127. See also Otto Michel, "Melchizedek," *TDNT,* 4:568-571.

On Melchizedek in the Dead Sea Scrolls see especially M. De Jonge and A. S. van der Woude, "11Q Melchizedek and the New Testament," *NTS* 12 (1966): 301-26 and A. S. van der Woude, "Melchizedek," *IDB-S,* pp. 585-6. For the view that Melchizedek in the Scrolls may be a member of the community see Jean Carmignac "Le document de Qumran sur Melkisedeq," *RevQ* 7 (1970): 343-78; Buchanan, *To the Hebrews,* 99-100, apparently agrees with Carmignac. See also Richard Longenecker, "The Melchizedek Argument of Hebrews," in *Unity and Diversity in New Testament Theology,* ed. Robert A. Guelich (Grand Rapids: Eerdmans, 1978), pp. 161-185.

51. *amētōr, apatōr, agenealogētos.* See Philo, *On Drunkenness,* 56-62; *On Abraham* 31; J. W. Thompson, *Beginnings of Christian Philosophy,* pp. 118-120.

52. Philo uses the word "unstained" *(amiantos)* of the Divine Word or Logos as ideal high priest, resident in the soul *(On Flight and Finding* 108-118; *The Special Laws* 1:113).

53. Behind "minister" is the Greek word *leitourgos,* used in 1:6 of angels. In 8:6 *leitourgia* is translated "ministry," and in 9:21 the same word stands behind "priestly service." In 10:11 *leitourgōn* (the present participle of the verb *leitourgeō*) is translated "at his service." *Leitourgikos* ("ministering") is used of angels in 1:14. On the word group see Rudolf Meyer and Hermann Strathmann, *TDNT* 4:215-231.

54. Philo expands on the allegorical significance of the furnishings, apparatus, and vestments of the temple, especially in *Life of Moses* 2.71-140. Luther rehearses numerous symbolic interpretations and then also offers his own allegorizing understanding: the Holy of Holies is the church triumphant, the Holy Place is the church militant, and the court is the synagogue. The lampstand with its seven branches signifies either the Word of God or the churches or the priests of the church or the consciences of individual persons. The ark of the covenant is Christ himself adorned on all sides with the heavenly gold of wisdom and grace.

55. *Paragenomenos* (from *paraginomai*) means "having appeared" or "having been revealed."

56. *Ephapax* (9:12; 10:10) is an emphatic form of *hapax,* and means "once for all," as *hapax* itself does in 9:26, 28; 10:2 (cf. Jude 2, 3). *Hapax* can mean simply "once": Christians were enlightened "once" (6:4); the high priest enters the

inner tent "once a year" *(hapax tou eniautou,* 9:7); God will shake earth and heaven "once more" or "one last time" *(eti hapax,* 9:26-27).

57. He entered not *di' haimatos tragōn* but *dia de tou idiou haimatos—dia* with the genitive to express attendant circumstances; compare Hebrews 13:22, *dia bracheōn* ("briefly"); Acts 15:32, *dia logou pollou* ("with much talk"); 2 Cor. 2:4, *dia pollōn dakrynōn* ("with many tears"). See C. F. D. Moule, *Idiom Book of New Testament Greek* (Cambridge: The University Press, 1971), p. 57.

58. On the red heifer see above all M. Parah and Appendix IV in *The Mishnah,* translated by Herbert Danby (London: Oxford University Press, 1933). Epistle of Barnabas 8 takes the heifer to signify Jesus. For Philo *(Special Laws* 1.261-272) the cleansing with the ashes of the red heifer speaks of the necessity of being purified by wisdom *(sophia)* and by the practice of virtues. That person may come with boldness to the sanctuary in order to present himself as victim, but that holy place is forbidden to the unholy.

59. *Diathēkē* can mean either "covenant" or "last will and testament." Scholars disagree concerning our author's usage: does he mean "covenant" or "will"? Is his usage consistent, or does he mean "covenant" in some contexts and "will" in others? Covenants were not ratified without animal sacrifices and wills do not take effect until the death of the testator. Thus a death is a necessary element in both arrangements.

60. "Shadow" *(skia)* stands in contrast to reality. In 8:5 and 9:23 *hypodeigma* ("copy" or "imitation") is a synonym for *skia.* Our author has several words for reality. In this same verse (10:1) he used *eikōn.* In 9:23 he speaks of "heavenly things" *(ta epourania).* In 1:3 he uses the word *hypostasis* to teach that the Son is the exact representation of "God's real being" *(BAGD),* to assert that Christ is the completely valid revelation of the transcendent reality of God (see Helmut Köster, *TDNT* 8:585-8). In Col. 2:17, *sōma* ("substance") is contrasted with *skia.* Elsewhere in Greek literature *alētheia* ("truth" or "reality") is a synonym for substance or transcendent and unchangeable things. On *skia* see Siegfried Schulz, *TDNT* 7:394-400.

61. *(egkainizō.)* See Johannes Behm, *TDNT* 3:453-4.

62. See 4:16 and note 35.

63. The text says literally, "Let us set our eyes upon one another for provoking *(paroxysmos)* to love and good deeds."

64. *Athlēsis* means literally an athletic "contest," and then by extension it means a "struggle" involving temptations and sufferings. The verb *athleō* is found in 2 Tim. 2:5; cf. 1 Clement 5:2. The Acts of Thomas (39) portrays Jesus as "the true and undefeated athlete" *(athlētēs).* Ignatius summoned Polycarp to endure martyrdom as "God's athlete" *(athlētēs),* Ignatius to Polycarp 2:3; cf. 3:2. Athletic metaphors occur also in 5:14 and 12:1-2. See note 46.

65. Behind "publicly exposed" is the Greek *theatrizomenoi.* "Spectacle" in 1 Cor. 4:9 renders *theatron.*

66. *Hypomonē* is "endurance, patience, perseverance, fortitude." *Hypomenō* means to "hold out, endure, remain, stand one's ground." The thought at the end of Chapter 10 is resumed in Chapter 12 where our author calls upon the readers to run their race "with fortitude or patience" just as Jesus "patiently endured" the cross (12:1-2). They must "endure" or "stand their ground" for the sake of discipline (12:7).

    Hebrews has many synonyms for "patience." "Faith" *(pistis)* is discussed in the following note. On "endurance" *(makrothymia)* see Heb. 6:12, 15 and note 48. In 3:6, 14 and 4:14 our author urges his readers to "hold fast" their confession and confidence (see note 28). In 11:27 our author uses *kartareō* to mean "to be strong or courageous or to endure."

67. Stephen Neill has commented on the way our author differs from both Paul and James in the use of the word *faith.* Paul looked to the past, to the promises of God and to their fulfillment in Jesus' death and resurrection, and defined faith as trust and acceptance directed at God's grace. James focused on faith in relation to the neighbor in the present and defined faith in its inseparable connection with the dynamic of obedience. The writer of Hebrews faced forward to the future, unknown and unguaranteed, and defined faith as hope and confidence, a synonym of all the words mentioned in the preceding note. See Stephen Neill, *Jesus Through Many Eyes* (Philadelphia: Fortress 1976), p. 108. Neill's summary smooths out many rough spots and simplifies a complex matter, but it is nonetheless useful. One thing Neill fails to capture is the upward (as well as the forward) movement of faith in Hebrews.

68. *pistei.* For a discussion of faith *(pistis)* and knowledge (gnōsis) in the ancient world, of the growing tendency to give faith an indispensable role in relation to the divine, of Philo's interpretation of faith as the bridge between the spiritual pilgrim and his true homeland, and of faith in Hebrews, see

especially J. W. Thompson, *Beginnings of Christian Philosophy*, 53-80; see also John Reumann, "Faith, Faithfulness in the New Testament," in *IDB* 5:332-5.

69. Helmut Koester interprets *hypostasis* (*TDNT* 8:572-589) not in the subjective sense of "conviction" assigned to the word by Luther but in the objective sense of "reality," that which is "underlying" in contrast to mere surface appearances (cf. 1:3). Koester understands 11:1 as declaring that the presence of the divine reality is found in the faith of the community.

Leonard Goppelt, in his *Theology of the New Testament* (Grand Rapids: Eerdmans, 1981-2), 2:262-5, tries to find a middle way and understands 11:1 to mean that faith is a standing firm in that which is hoped for, partly on the basis of a comparison with 3:14, where *hypostasis* is used in a context which describes faith as the opposite of falling away.

A comparison between 10:1 and 11:1 is helpful. 10:1 says that the law has only a shadow (*skia*) of the good things to come. 11:1 announces that in contrast to the law, and to the cult based on that law, faith grasps the reality (not the shadow or appearance only) of the things we hope for.

70. *Martyreō* means in the active voice "to bear witness" or "testify" and in the passive voice "to be approved" or "to have witness borne" by someone about something. *Martyrion* (3:5) is "testimony" or "proof." *Martys* is "a witness." See BAGD.

71. "What is seen *(to blepomenon)* was made out of things which do not appear" *(mē ek phainomenon)*. Philo, standing in a long tradition of Greek philosophy, calls the visible, physical world "the phenomenal world," the world of appearance. God the Creator is *aphanēs*, unseen and invisible. *(On the Creation* 45; *On Husbandry* 42; *On the Confusion of Tongues* 172; *On the Migration of Abraham* 105, 179).

72. Luther comments that Abel "when he was alive could not teach his one brother . . . (but) now that he is dead, that is, lives far more vigorously, teaches the whole world. So great a thing is faith, that is, life in God." Philo also has the tradition that "Abel, therefore, strange as it seems, has both been put to death and lives" (*The Worse Attacks the Better* 48; cf. 69-70).

73. *(chrematizō)*. The Wise Men (Matt. 2:12) and Joseph (Matt. 2:22) were "warned by God" in dreams. It was "divinely revealed" to Simeon that he should see the Christ (Luke 2:26),

and Cornelius was "informed" or "directed" by an angel to send for Peter (Acts 10:22).

74. *Dynamin elaben eis katabolēn spermatos* is literally "received power for the sowing of seed."

75. The nominative "Sarah herself" as subject (read by RSV) is *autē Sarra.* The dative, as suggested by the alternative translation, is exactly the same in Greek except for the addition of an iota subscript. See Moffatt and Bruce and *BAGD.* Following the alternative (reading the dative) might seem to be a happy solution, but Philo offers support for the notion that Sarah herself, though a woman, sows seed. In Philo's writings Sarah represents virtue which brings divine wisdom to Abraham (*Allegorical Interpretation* 2.82; *On the Cherubim* 9; *The Preliminary Studies* 22-23). Therefore in this case Philo says that Sarah sows the seeds of correct instruction in Abraham. "In bodily marriage the male sows the seed and the female receives it; on the other hand, in the matings within the soul, though virtue seemingly ranks as wife, her natural function is to sow good counsels and excellent words and to inculcate tenets truly profitable to life" (*On Abraham* 101; cf. *On Flight and Finding* 51-52). See Sidney Sowers, *The Hermeneutics of Philo and Hebrews* (Richmond: 1965), pp. 134f.

76. Philo represents all the wise men and women of Scripture as sojourners: "To them the heavenly region, where their citizenship lies, is their native land; the earthly region in which they became sojourners is a foreign country" (*The Confusion of Tongues* 77-78). Indeed life in the body is that of a sojourner in a foreign land. Heaven or God himself is our country, kinsfolk, hearth, and wealth (*Who Is the Heir* 26-27). The migration of Abraham from Ur to Canaan was an outward symbol of Abraham's (and every wise person's) real journey: from flesh to spirit, from the material to the intelligible world.

77. Human beings are born into this world "as into a foreign city," writes Philo. We are "aliens and sojourners" here until the end of our life (*On the Cherubim* 120-1; *On Husbandry* 65). Sometimes in Philo Jerusalem is named as the real or native city of the soul, or the Divine Logos is called the noblest city of refuge (*On Flight and Finding* 97).

78. *Proskairon* means "fleeting" or "temporary." The "fleeting" is all that is in the grip of this world and belongs to the earth. Here we have no "lasting" city (*menousa* from *menein,* "to remain, endure, abide," 13:14). Heaven and earth are the

material works of God's hands, and they will perish; only the divine reality itself abides, remains *(diamenein,* 1:10-11).

Everything earthly grows old, becomes obsolete and passes away—even the first covenant (1:11; 8:13). Everything that belongs to that first covenant, including the tabernacle, is made by humans (8:2), made with hands (9:24), tangible (12:18), and will pass away with this present world.

As for the opposite of "fleeting," our author has many words for that which is lasting, heavenly, eternal. God's throne is "for ever" *(eis ton aiōna tou aiōnios,* 1:8). The Lord is "the same" *(ho autos,* 1:12; 13:8). The Son is priest "for ever" *(eis ton aiōna,* 5:6; 6:20; 7:17, 20, 24). He is priest "continually" or "for all time" *(eis to diēnekēs,* 7:3) and has perfected "for all time" by a single offering those who are consecrated (10:12, 14). He is able to save "for all time" *(eis to pantelēs,* 7:25) and he lives "always" *(pantote,* 7:25). He has secured an "eternal" *(aiōnios)* redemption (9:12) and is mediator of a new and "eternal" inheritance (9:15). He has made a single offering ("once for all"). See note 56. A pilgrim people looks for a reality that has foundations (11:10), and is "better," "heavenly" (11:16) or "of God" (12:22), and "unshakeable" (12:28).

79. On the mantle of the prophets see 1 Kings 19:13, 19; 2 Kings 1:8; Zech. 12:4; Mark 1:6; 1 Clement 17:1; Ascension of Isaiah 2:7-10.

80. Moffatt, p. 191, quotes Paulinus of Nola, *Letters* 38:3, but says that this mystical sense of the participation of Christ in the sufferings of patriarchs and prophets is no part of our author's thinking. On the participation of Christ in the sufferings of ancients see Melito, *On Pascha,* passim.

81. *Toigaroun,* used only here and at 1 Thess. 4:8 in the New Testament.

82. *(aphoraō: apo-horaō).* 4 Macc. 17:10.

83. *Euperistatos* means "ensnaring," "closely clinging." *Euperispastos* is "distracting."

84. *(hypomonē).* See discussion on 10:36 and note 66.

85. See Martin Hengel, *Crucifixion* (Philadelphia: Fortress Press, 1977).

86. The preposition is *anti.*

87. *Eklyō* in the passive means to "grow slack" or "lose heart."

88. Literally the text reads, "You have not yet resisted as far as blood" *(BAGD).* The phrase may mean loss of life or suffering

wounds in combat. The latter seems likely. *TDNT* 1:173.

89. *(episkopeō)*.

90. Is Hebrews dominated by Platonic, spatial dualism or by apocalyptic, temporal dualism? For a rapid review of the debate and for an exegesis of 12:18-29 see J. W. Thompson, *Beginnings of Christian Philosophy*, pp. 41-52. Thompson argues persuasively that the author of Hebrews received an apocalyptically and temporally oriented tradition and that in appropriating it, he edited or redacted it, stamping it with his own Platonic, dualistic outlook.

For the view that the apocalyptic or eschatological element is dominant see Otto Michel's commentary; Otovied Hofius, *Katapausis: Die Vorstellung von endzeitlichen Ruheort im Hebraerbrief* (Tübingen: J. C. B. Mohr, 1970); Ronald Williamson, *Philo and the Epistle to the Hebrews* (Leiden: E. J. Brill, 1970); C. K. Barrett, "The Eschatology of the Epistle to the Hebrews," in W. D. Davies and D. Daube, *The Background of the New Testament and Its Eschatology* (Cambridge: The University Press, 1956), pp. 363-93; William Manson, *The Epistle to the Hebrews* (London: Hodder & Stoughton, 1951).

Many older and newer writers regard Hebrews as fundamentally Platonic in its outlook, interpreting the past and present in terms of the notion that the visible world is only an imperfect and shadowy imitation or copy of the real and eternal world. See Moffatt in his commentary and Ernest F. Scott, *The Varieties of New Testament Religion* (New York: Scribner, 1944), among older writers.

91. Hebrews 12:18-24 is crucial for G. W. Buchanan's understanding of Hebrews. He takes "heavenly Jerusalem" to mean the actual, historical capital city of the promised land. It is "heavenly," not because it is in heaven, but because it has been divinely chosen. "Innumerable angels" hovered over Jerusalem at every "festal gathering." The "first-born who are enrolled in heaven" are the members of the earthly Christian community who gathered especially on the Day of Atonement and New Year's Day. They were not ex-Qumraners but a celibate community of Christians formed of Diaspora Jews who had come to live near Mount Zion at Jerusalem. On the great solemn festival days God was with them and among them as "Judge of all." If the sacrifices were properly performed, then "the spirits of just men" were indeed "made perfect." This Christian community thought of Jesus' death not as a

criminal execution occurring in connection with Passover in the spring, as our gospels report it, but as an atoning sacrifice in closest relation to the Day of Atonement and the New Year's Festival in the fall. There in Jerusalem the purified saints await the inheritance. "The rest" they seek is the land of Canaan itself. Buchanan, pp. 221-7.

92. On the meaning of "drawing near" or "approaching" (12:18, 22) as the action of a convert or proselyte or a movement of a worshiper or priest toward a sanctuary, see commentary on 4:16, note 35.

93. Buchanan, pp. 228-233.

94. Buchanan, pp. 256, 267.

95. "Do not be led astray" or "do not be carried or swept away" (*mē parapheresthē*, from *para-pherō*) suggests the same picture as "drift away" or "be carried away" (*pararyōmen*, 2:2), the fate of those who have no anchor (6:9), who fail to "hold fast" their confidence and confession (3:6, 14; 6:11; 10:23) and so do not endure (see commentary on 10:23). Another way to express the opposite of drifting away or being carried away is to speak of the heart's being "strengthened" or "secured" (*bebaiousthai*, 13:9). See note 16.

96. Exodus 33:7 says that "Moses pitched his tent outside the camp." Philo interpreted that to mean that the soul which loves God abandons the encumbrances of bodily things and makes virtue its dwelling place (*Allegorical Interpretation* 2:54-55; 3.46; *The Worse Attacks the Better* 160). For Philo and our author, "outside the camp" (*exō tēs parembolēs*) means beyond the earthly sphere. Hence Jesus' sacrifice is offered not merely on earth near Jerusalem but in the heavenly sphere, and Christians are called to go "outside the camp" by giving up earthly securities, by living as strangers and pilgrims and not simply by going outside Judaism, for example. See Joachim Jeremias, "pylē," *TDNT* 6:921-2.

97. *Hegoumenos*, "one who leads," is present participle of *hegeomai*, "I lead, guide." "One who serves" (*diakonōn*) is antonym in Luke 22:26. The word is used of political officials (Matt. 2:6; Acts 7:10), military commanders (1 Macc. 9:30; 1 Clement 37:2-3), and religious leaders (Heb. 13:7, 17, 24; Acts 14:12; 15:22; 1 Clement 1:3).

98. *An-agō* means to "lead or bring up." See Rom. 10:7; Tobit 13:12; Ps. 30:3.

99. (*dia bracheōn epesteila hymin*).

100. (*apolyō*). See *BAGD* for discussion and references.